Managing Your Ca
Education Adn

Universities into the 21st Century

Series Editors: Noel Entwistle and Roger King

Managing Your Career in Higher Education Administration

Michelle Gander

Heather Moyes

Emma Sabzalieva

First published 2014 by
PALGRAVE MACMILLAN

Palgrave Macmillan in the UK is an imprint of Macmillan Publishers Limited,
registered in England, company number 785998, of Houndmills, Basingstoke,
Hampshire RG21 6XS.

Palgrave Macmillan in the US is a division of St Martin's Press LLC,
175 Fifth Avenue, New York, NY 10010.

Palgrave Macmillan is the global academic imprint of the above companies
and has companies and representatives throughout the world.

Palgrave® and Macmillan® are registered trademarks in the United States,
the United Kingdom, Europe and other countries.

ISBN 978–1–137–32832–8

This book is printed on paper suitable for recycling and made from fully
managed and sustained forest sources. Logging, pulping and manufacturing
processes are expected to conform to the environmental regulations of the
country of origin.

A catalogue record for this book is available from the British Library.

A catalog record for this book is available from the Library of Congress.

Printed in China

MG – For Marcus, for keeping me out of my own head and making me go running

HM – For Bethan and Anwen, my higher education administrators in training, and Martin, my very own academic

ES – For my husband, Asad, and children, Aliya and Maxad: with love, always

Contents

Figures and Tables

Figure

Tables

Foreword

When Heather Moyes told me that she and colleagues from her MBA programme were collaborating on a book about careers in higher education administration, I was over the moon. This is a book our profession has been waiting for a very long time. Much has been written about academic careers in higher education, but there has been no comprehensive go-to text for university administrators. Finally, we have it in *Managing Your Career in Higher Education Administration*. The authors have reclaimed the words 'administrator' and 'administration' through an exploration of the shift from administration done by academics to administration done by administrators whose fundamental role is to facilitate our academics to be brilliant teachers and researchers and our students to achieve their potential and ambitions.

The increasing specialisation of higher education administration has been a necessary response to the increasing complexity of the external world in which we operate and to some extent has come at the expense of broad and deep understanding of the purpose of a university and of the role of the administration within it. We have all at times been challenged to explain what 'all those people with complicated job titles' actually do and to resist accusations that the 'bureaucrats have taken over the asylum'. Successful universities recognise, and are proud of, how their academic and administrative communities work seamlessly and with mutual respect to achieve their organisations' shared goals.

Managing Your Career in Higher Education Administration provides an accessible overview of the history and purpose of universities before presenting a wealth of theoretical understanding and practical information to situate the changing role of the administration and to support administrators in developing their careers from first point of entry to reaching the highest levels. Personal case studies add depth and meaning to the theory and practical tips. This is a book that can be read cover to cover or dipped in and out of, depending on the reader's needs and interests. Each chapter ends with follow-up references and links to additional tools to support personal and professional development planning.

As the current Vice-Chair of the Association of University Administrators (AUA), I hope *Managing Your Career in Higher Education Administration* provides a timely and highly visible reminder of the critical role of administrators in making our universities the successful organisations they are. But more than that it reminds each of us that we are individually responsible for our development at whatever level we are. At a time of significant resource constraints in our institutions when staff development funding is often severely restricted, this book shows that we can do much ourselves through joining already established networks like the AUA and building networks in and across our institutions.

It has been a privilege to contribute to this important text, and I look forward to the buzz that it will create in our sector in the UK and beyond. This is the go-to text for anyone working in or thinking about working in higher education administration. I very much hope academic colleagues will find the book equally instructive and that we will all accept the call to action to take personal responsibility for deepening our understanding of the complex world in which we operate, broadening our understanding of what it means to work in a university and investing time and energy in our professional networks and relationships as we plan and navigate our higher education careers.

Tessa Harrison
Registrar, University of Southampton
Vice-Chair, Association of University Administrators
October 2013

Acknowledgements

The germ of the idea for this book emerged one evening in 2011 as three students from the Institute for Education, University of London's MBA in Higher Education Management dared to imagine a life without essay deadlines and syndicate tasks. Tired, but also enthused about what higher education is for and about why working in universities is a wonderful thing, we knew this was the sector in which we wanted to pursue our careers. But we were less sure of what that really meant: what might a career in higher education administration look like and how much influence could we have over our own career path? We knew how we'd got to where we were – through a mixture of accident and design, with a good dash of serendipity and fair bit of hard work along the way.

But how had all those people in more senior positions around the sector got to where they were? If we wanted to continue to feel fulfilled and challenged in our work, whatever that might look like for each of us, were we doing the right things? Or were there some tricks that we were missing? The obvious solution – read a book – was not available, at least not one that dealt with the particular opportunities and challenges of carving out a career in university administration. So we decided to write one ourselves and, through that process, to reflect upon what we'd learned so far and what others were willing to share with us.

We are extremely grateful to Palgrave Macmillan for enabling us to turn our idea into reality, to our interviewees for giving us their time and sharing their experiences with us, to our colleagues for their encouragement and comments on drafts and to our institutions, The Open University, Cardiff University and the University of Oxford, for their support. Thanks, too, to our three anonymous reviewers, whose feedback helped us greatly in shaping and balancing the content of this book. And thank goodness for the MBA in Higher Education Management and the Association of University Administrators, through which we were able to make so many connections. Lastly, a heartfelt thank you to our families for offering us the time and space to pursue this project.

The authors would like to thank Taylor and Francis (www.tandf online.com) for giving permission to reproduce the table on p. 56; Open Universiteit for giving permission to reproduce the material on p. 70; and Leadership Foundation for Higher Education for giving permission to reproduce the material on p. 78.

Series Editors' Preface

The series is designed to fill a niche between publications about universities and colleges that focus exclusively on the practical concerns of university teachers, managers or policy makers and those which are written with an academic, research-based audience in mind that provide detailed evidence, argument and conclusions. The books in this series are intended to build upon evidence and conceptual frameworks in discussing issues which are of direct interest to those concerned with universities. The issues in the series will cover a broad range, from the activities of teachers and students to wider developments in policy, at local, national and international levels.

The current pressures on academic and administrative staff, and university managers, mean that, only rarely, can they justify the time needed to read lengthy descriptions of research findings. The aim, therefore, is to produce compact, readable books that in many parts provide a synthesis and overview of often seemingly disparate issues.

Some of the books, such as the first in the series – *The University in the Global Age*, are deliberatively broad in focus and conceptualisation, looking at the system as a whole in an international perspective, and are a collection of integrated chapters, written by specialist authors. In other books, such as *Research and Teaching: Beyond the Divide*, the author looks within universities at a specific issue to examine what constitutes 'best practice' through a lens of available theory and research evidence.

Underpinning arguments, where appropriate with research-based conceptual analysis, make the books more convincing to an academic audience, whilst the link to 'good practice and policy' avoids the remoteness that comes from an over-abstract approach. The series will thus appeal not just to those working within higher education, but also to a wider audience interested in knowing more about an organisation that is attracting increasing government and media attention.

NOEL ENTWISTLE
ROGER KING

About the Authors

Michelle Gander, Heather Moyes and Emma Sabzalieva met whilst studying for the Institute of Education (IoE), University of London's MBA in Higher Education Management. The authors are all established higher education administrators with extensive experience gained in a range of roles and higher education settings. This is their first collaboration.

Michelle Gander is currently Head of the University Secretary's Office at The Open University, UK, where she has worked in a variety of posts since 1999. She is on the editorial advisory board of the Association of University Administrator's (AUA) journal, *Perspectives*; is a specialist assessor for the AUA's postgraduate certificate in professional practice; and is a trustee for the British School of Osteopathy. She writes and blogs on women's equality issues.

Heather Moyes has worked at Cardiff University, UK, since 2007, taking up the post of Business Manager for the Student Experience and Academic Standards portfolio in the Vice Chancellor's Office in September 2013. She has also worked at Lancaster University and the University of Salford, UK. She is currently AUA's Branch Advocate for Cardiff University and is a trustee of NewLink Wales, a substance misuse charity.

Emma Sabzalieva is College Registrar at St Antony's College, University of Oxford, UK, and since joining the university in 2007 has worked in both central teams and colleges. She started her career working for the University of Central Asia in Tajikistan and now does independent research on higher education and social change in Central Asia. She is also Chair of Governors at a state primary school.

1 Introduction

▶ Why you should read this book

For people already working in higher education administration, this book will help you develop an effective career in the sector by offering practical advice and real-life guidance with a theoretical underpinning. It is relevant whether you are in your first job looking ahead or you are an established manager reflecting on your own professional development and that of your team. We believe that if you want to – and we think you should want to – you can make a career in higher education administration.

The book also aims to encourage people who don't currently work in the sector – whether you are a university student thinking about your next steps, or you have initially pursued a career in another sector and are thinking about a career change – to consider higher education administration as a fulfilling and exciting career choice.

Until now, nobody has written a book specifically for people working in higher education administration who want to understand what their career prospects are and how they can go about developing a career in this sector. The sheer diversity of roles and the lack of a typical job profile help explain why it's difficult to pin down what exactly it means to be a higher education administrator. One careers guidance website offers the following wide-ranging list of possible roles:

> Administrators may have student recruitment, funding, quality assurance, marketing, or public relations roles; or they may be responsible for budgetary/financial administration, project management or human resources management. Many work in a general capacity – undertaking tasks from all of these areas.   (Target Jobs, 2013)

Despite the diversity, higher education administration can be seen to be a distinct sphere of activity. In the UK alone, the Higher Education Statistics Agency shows that there were more than 200,000[1] people working in administrative roles in UK higher education institutions in 2011–2012 (HESA, 2013). That represents 38% of the workforce, with academic staff making up 47% of the total; yet you can find a range of books (including one in this series) on developing an academic career. In the USA, the split for that year showed 51% of employees working in degree-granting institutions in roles that encompass the full range of administration and support functions (United States Census Bureau, 2012). That equates to well over two million people working in administration in both public and private higher education institutions. Whilst the Australian and Canadian censuses don't offer information at such a granular level, both systems recognise university administration as a category of staff (in Canada: 'Administrators – post-secondary education and vocational training').

▶ Can you have a career in higher education administration?

Have you ever seen a careers fair stand promoting higher education administration as a career? Did you grow up dreaming about being a higher education administrator and not a doctor, teacher or pilot? If there is one thing that binds many of those who have worked in higher education administration for some time, it's a sense of surprise that we got here in the first place, that we're still here and that this is, indeed, a place where you can build and develop a rewarding working life. In part, this may stem from a lack of realisation that there is anything particularly different about universities as workplaces.

But once in the sector, you can find opportunities and you can progress within and between organisations. The senior higher education administrators we interviewed for this book all told us that you *can* forge a career in higher education administration. There are parts of the sector which are emergent or not yet fully embedded (in the UK, for example, development/fundraising or student visa compliance officers), and these areas present even greater career opportunities because there isn't yet a strong core of people out there with directly related experience.

How to get into higher education administration: entry routes
The good news if you don't currently work in higher education administration is that there are multiple entry points into the sector.

Joining at an early career stage
It is quite common for people to join universities with limited work experience (say, less than five years), often at a relatively low level

within the organisation. Some will have come from other public and voluntary sector organisations, but others join from the private sector. Like many people, Tessa Harrison, now Registrar of Southampton University, wasn't sure what to do when she finished university and, in her words, 'ended up working in a solicitor's office and I was absolutely rubbish!' So after a short time, she looked around at local employers and found an administrative job at the university where her husband had just started a degree. The experience she gained at Anglia Polytechnic (now Anglia Ruskin) University enabled her to move after just four years to become Head of the Undergraduate Registry at Lancaster University, progressing in due course to lead the Quality Assurance Unit there. She became Academic Registrar at the University of the West of England in 2006, joining Southampton in 2011. Similarly, Jon Baldwin worked his way up to being Deputy Vice Chancellor (Professional Services) at Murdoch University in Australia, having begun his career in clerical work for local government before moving into higher education to become an administrative assistant at what was then Preston Polytechnic.

Graduate training programmes

A small number of UK universities offer graduate training schemes as an entry point to university administration. These are commonly one-to-two-year fixed-term appointments, involving rotations between roles in a number of different departments. Whilst they don't usually guarantee a permanent job at the end, the reality is that people coming from these schemes are highly likely both to find opportunities and to continue employment in the higher education sector. Imperial College London has been running a Management Training Scheme since 1998, and in 2013, it introduced a Finance Training Scheme, offering a more specialist route into higher education administration.

In addition to individual university initiatives, the concept of graduate training – which is already common in other sectors and a popular route for university graduates – is becoming more embedded in the UK. Chapter 3 looks at what the Association of Heads of University Administration's 2012-launched university leadership programme, Ambitious Futures, can offer graduates as a springboard into a career in the sector.

Transferring from another industry

Becoming a university administrator midway through your career is probably the most challenging point at which to switch over. Part of the challenge can be convincing the university you are applying to work in that your skills are transferable enough to make up for lack of direct experience. Another significant challenge is a financial risk, in that – as the example below shows – you may effectively be restarting your career and joining at a lower level than the industry you are leaving.

Tania Rhodes-Taylor, now Director of Marketing and Communications at Queen Mary, University of London, worked in marketing for many years in the private sector in the UK and Hong Kong. She was able to take a much more junior role at a charity in the UK only because voluntary redundancy from the private company gave her the financial stability to do so for a short time. However, Rhodes-Taylor was prepared to make this move because of her desire to shift career track and move into education. Taking this step down the career ladder in terms of seniority set her on a different track, and she progressed steadily to more senior marketing and communications roles from the charity to a Department for Education project, to the Institute of Education, University of London, and from there to her current role at Queen Mary.

Transferring over from academia

It's not a myth: you can find staff in higher education administration who began their working life as academics and actively chose to switch career tack. But working in higher education administration is not the 'easy option' for aspiring academics who aren't able to make it as an academic. Rather, where former academics are successful in administration, it's because of active choices they make about the direction of their career.

Andrew West, Director of Student Services at Sheffield University, started his career as a doctoral student researching medieval monasticism. He explains that doing a PhD gave him a greater affinity to higher education as a sector. His desire to work in the public sector coupled with a feeling that 'I'd had enough of living in the fourteenth century' during his research led to a career at Sheffield that has taken in 'about ten different roles – I've rather lost count now, but in the area of academic administration, student administration and then latterly, broader roles in student services and now incorporating student recruitment'.

It's also possible, though less common, for administrators to become academics and – these days more commonly – for both administrators and academics to take on 'blended' or 'third space' roles. In Chapter 2, we discuss these ideas in more detail, as well as how critically important it is for higher education administrators to understand what our purpose is – with that same purpose applying regardless of how you got into the sector.

▶ Administrator, manager, professional services, non-academics...

When planning this book, we took the conscious decision to talk about administrators and administration. Universities in the UK use a variety of terminologies to talk about the people who work in universities, and after deliberation, we felt that 'administrator' was the best choice. We decided not to use 'manager' or 'management' for two reasons: firstly, because not everyone working in higher education manages people or services and one of the key groups of people we're aiming at in the book are people at a fairly early stage in their career. Secondly, there can be something of a stigma attached to talking about yourself as a university manager, especially if you're talking to academic colleagues: it has ramifications of control and autocracy that sit uncomfortably for some (see also Chapter 5). We also turned down 'professional services' and 'non-academic', the former because it suggests that some services are not professional, and the latter because it creates a negative identity. In her 2011 follow-up to a 2004 study, Szekeres observes that the 'naming issue' is still a source of frustration to what she calls professional staff in Australian universities, identifying that terms such as 'non-academic' or 'support' can feel denigrating.

But the choice of 'administrator' was not because it was the only term left after ruling out other options! We also looked at the way that professional associations for people working in higher education identify themselves. In the UK, two key groups are the Association of University Administrators and the Association of Heads of University Administration. Both groups have had periodic debate about nomenclature and both have ultimately decided to use 'administrator'. One of the most active relevant discussion boards on LinkedIn is the American-run group 'Higher education administration', which has over 20,000 members. In fact, if you look up 'administration', it not only defines us as 'the people responsible for running a business, organization, etc'. but gives as an example of the noun in use 'the university administration took their demands seriously' (Oxford Dictionaries, undated)! Our use of 'administrator' is not meant to be limited, for example, to course administrators or student finance administrators, but encompasses the wide variety of supporting roles in universities, from Estates to Libraries, from Finance to Human Resources.

And whilst we're defining our terms, we should be clear that the book refers to higher/post-secondary education in a university setting, although we recognise that higher education can be found in other places too, increasingly in further education.

▶ About the case studies

Throughout the book, you will see thoughts and reflections from a range of senior higher education administrators. By 'senior' we mean colleagues who have progressively taken on more responsibility, for example, for people, functions or projects and are now at a stage in their career where they lead and manage a significant functional area and/or are accountable for one or more of their universities' strategic priorities.

We selected people working in a variety of roles, mainly at UK universities, although some either work in other countries or have experience of other settings, and interviewed them in 2013 specifically for this book. Most of the interviewees were undertaken face-to-face and lasted about an hour, but we also interviewed by phone, Skype and email. Some of our interviewees (e.g. the Vice Chancellor of The Open University) were only posed a subset of the full list of questions as we wanted to ask them about a specific area of their knowledge or expertise. The methodology selected for the longer interviews was semi-structured, meaning that we started with a pre-agreed list of topics and themes to cover but had the flexibility to tailor the questions as other ideas and discussions arose (see Lewis-Beck et al., 2004 for more on qualitative and other research methods).

Our case studies were selected by the authors to offer a snapshot of the diversity within the sector: institutional type, regional location, role group, individual background and outlook and so on. Through these indicators we not only aimed to create as balanced a picture as possible, but also quite consciously aimed to interview as many senior women as possible. It is still the case that staff at lower levels are more likely to be women – for example, 80% of staff classified as 'administrators' in English higher education institutions in 2010–2011 were women (more senior categories include 'manager' – 53% women, 'non-academic professionals' – 59% women and 'technician' – 34% women) (HEFCE, 2012). So, by including senior women in our case studies, we hope to show how it is possible for women to progress and flourish in higher education administration. Gander (2010) discusses in further detail the ongoing gender gap in higher education, focussing on senior administrators.

The case studies enhance what we have to say by offering real-life examples of, for instance, how problems have been solved or how they have made decisions through their career. Not all the interviewees feature in every chapter, so here is a summary:

Name	Position (at time of interview)	University (at time of interview)
Jon Baldwin*	Deputy Vice Chancellor, Professional Services	Murdoch University, Australia
Martin Bean*	Vice Chancellor	The Open University, UK
Alan Burrell	Estates Director	The Open University, UK
Tracy Carlton	Head of Product Development	The Open University, UK
Michael Di Grappa*	Vice President, Administration and Finance	McGill University, Canada
Jayne Dowden	Director of Human Resources	Cardiff University, UK
Liesl Elder	Director of Development	Oxford University, UK
Kirsten Gillingham	Bursar	St Antony's College, Oxford University, UK
Paul Greatrix	Registrar	University of Nottingham, UK
Tessa Harrison	Registrar	University of Southampton, UK
Hugh Jones	Chief Operating Officer	Cardiff University, UK
Sarah Randall-Paley	Director of Finance	Lancaster University, UK
Tania Rhodes-Taylor	Director of Marketing and Communications	Queen Mary University of London, UK
Mark Swindlehurst	Director of Facilities	Lancaster University, UK
Andrew West	Director of Student Services	University of Sheffield, UK
Amanda Wilcox	Senior Advisor, Pro-Vice-Chancellors' Office	University of Hull, UK

An asterisk next to an interviewee's name indicates that their interview followed the more condensed format described above.

Everyone we interviewed has given their permission for their full names to be used and has had the opportunity to review any direct quotes we use in the book. We are incredibly grateful to everyone who agreed to be interviewed, for giving up their time to speak with us and for allowing us to use their views and pass on their advice.

▶ Expertise from the UK and beyond

Whilst the book draws primarily on expertise and experience from the UK higher education administration sector, there is no doubt that the issues we discuss have relevance to other countries too. To add value for those readers, both inside and outside the UK, who might be thinking internationally for their career development, we have included some material about non-UK settings and from the perspective of other countries. Jon Baldwin, for example, moved from the UK to Australia as a way of developing his career after being Registrar at Warwick University and holding similar positions at other British universities. As he says, 'coming to a new country, I got the opportunity [to work in] a different culture, a different context, different politics, different styles [and that] seemed to me to be a really interesting thing to do'.

Our international approach has focussed on higher education environments with similarities to the UK sector, in particular Australia, Canada and the USA. Yet our research for the book undertaken on the social media-enabled network LinkedIn (see Chapter 4) engaged commentators not just from those countries but from sectors as diverse as Albania and India, suggesting that the book offers valuable insights for people who might be considering a move into a British university or who want to learn more about higher education administration in the UK.

▶ Getting the most out of the book

We'd suggest using the book in one of two ways. It is structured in such a way that you can read it from start to finish, or you can dip into it at various times to help you with a particular question you might have, as well as a skills/knowledge gap you are seeking to address. Each chapter has a particular focus which combines practical advice, theory from higher education literature and suggestions for how you can take your own learning or reflection forward. Regardless of the approach you take, the chapters are designed to be equally applicable to a graduate trainee as to someone considering a mid-career change. Your own needs and interests will determine the individualised action you take as a result of reading the book.

In Chapter 2, we lay the foundations for the book by examining the concept of a university: what is the 'idea' of the university and what are universities for? We argue that, regardless of your career stage or whether you plan to stay working in higher education administration for the next year or for the rest of your working life, it's fundamentally important to have a sound understanding of why universities do what they do and why they do it in the (often rather unique) way that they do. We look at whether higher education administration is becoming a 'profession', and why having an 'idea' of higher education administration is valuable for administrators in both generalised and specialised role groups.

Chapters 3 and 4 focus on personal and professional development areas over which you as an individual have more control. In a simplistic way, these look at 'what you know' and 'who you know' – but, of course, there's much more to it than that. Chapter 3 helps you understand how you can develop your skills and experience, focussing particularly on formal qualifications and continuing professional development. We also examine other tools and experiences you can gain, both inside higher education and more broadly. Chapter 4 explores how you can use your networks to create opportunities. We look at why networks are important, which networking types can be effective for higher education administrators, how you can add value to your networks and why you need to manage your networks pro-actively.

In Chapter 5, we move on to consider the role of the manager and management in higher education administration. This chapter is both for people who are managed by others and for people who are managers themselves. We look at different types of management relationships that are unique to higher education, offer advice and guidance on what it takes to be a good manager in our setting and suggest strategies you can use to get the most out of your relationship with your manager.

Two career development tools that can be used by and for managers are then explored in Chapter 6, which focusses on coaching and mentoring, specifically from the viewpoint of higher education administration. We discuss the differences in the two approaches, when each might be most useful and the perceived beneficial outcomes.

The book is drawn together by the concluding chapter (Chapter 7). We discuss some of the many choices you may be confronted with at various points in your career, including the choice about whether you do, in fact, want to pursue a career in higher education administration. We draw on the authors' own experiences and choices to depict our own career maps as an example of how you can develop quite different job paths within universities. We look at some of the senior roles towards which you could aspire, as well as at some of the factors that may, at various times in your life, both help and hinder your own pathway.

It is our intention in this book to show that you can pursue a fulfilling and interesting career in higher education administration, whatever your personal circumstances, provided that you are prepared to take an active role in your personal and professional development. Higher education around the world is perennially shifting, changing as a result of internal and sector-led developments as well as external pressures, and this will no doubt have implications for higher education administration as a career choice – we expect, for example, that topics such as shared services and outsourcing will become more prevalent in the coming years. But on the other hand, universities and higher education providers have existed for hundreds of years and show no sign of dissipating. Where there are universities, there need to be administrators. And, as a higher education administrator, you have the opportunity to be part of something much bigger, and that will never cease to be challenging, exciting and rewarding.

▶ Note

1   Includes full-time, part-time and atypical staff in the following role categories: 'managers', 'non-academic professionals', 'student welfare workers, careers advisors, vocational training instructors, personnel and planning officers', 'artistic, media, public relations, marketing and sports occupations', 'library assistants, clerks and general administrative assistants', and 'secretaries, typists, receptionists and telephonists'.

▶ References

Gander, M. A. (2010) 'Cracked but not broken', *Perspectives: Policy and Practice in Higher Education*, 14(4), 120–126.

HEFCE (18 July 2012) Staff employed at HEFCE-funded HEIs: Trends and profiles 1995–96 to 2010–11, www.hefce.ac.uk/data/year/2012/201214/, accessed 25 June 2013.

HESA (17 January 2013) Staff at Higher Education Institutions in the UK 2011/12 (SFR 1850), http://www.hesa.ac.uk/index.php?option=com_content&task=view&id=2662&Itemid=161, accessed 25 November 2013.

Lewis-Beck, M. A., Bryman, A. and Liao, T. F. (2004) *The Sage Encyclopaedia of Social Science Research Methods*, London: Sage Publications.

Oxford Dictionaries (undated) http://oxforddictionaries.com/definition/english/administration?q=administration, accessed 24 June 2013.

Target Jobs (2013) Higher education administrator: Job description, http://targetjobs.co.uk/careers-advice/job-descriptions/279775-higher-education-administrator-job-description, accessed 25 November 2013.

United States Census Bureau (2012) Employees in higher education by sex and occupation (296), http://www.census.gov/compendia/statab/cats/education/higher_education_finances_fees_and_staff.html, accessed 25 November 2013.

2 Working in a University

▶ Introduction

This chapter is about what working in universities is like for those employed in what we are defining broadly as the 'administration' – and why. What, if anything, is distinctive about higher education institutions as places of work (and are you a good fit for that environment)? What are the joys and tribulations, the opportunities and risks, of the higher education context and what might that mean for your working life, be that on a day-to-day level or over the longer-term trajectory of your career? What is the place of the administration within universities today? In addressing these questions, we focus primarily on the British context; however, many of the themes we explore are not country-specific and will have relevance beyond the UK.

So, why would anyone other than academics want to work in a university? One thing all the people we interviewed for this book shared was a passion for what they did. The following three accounts are typical of what we heard:

> Universities are interesting places. It's a challenge, but it's also part of the fun to know that you're working with incredibly bright people who are driving forward the bounds of knowledge, doing innovative research, who are also engaged in developing the brightest part of the population – the students. As a professional, I would find it very difficult to go and work in another industry now because you wouldn't get that level of stimulation.   (Jayne Dowden)

> Working with the biggest innovators in the world – incredible ideas, incredibly intelligent people – is just so exciting. And the students, that's the other thing that's really exciting. Being with young people who are just at the start of a really big journey and who are discovering amazing stuff and their own potentials – that's really exciting.   (Kirsten Gillingham)

> It's a brilliant sector to work in and from a point of view of having value to society, it must be one of those ones which is hard to beat.

And for me the underpinning purpose is my benchmark rationale I suppose. So I suppose my advice would be: if that is something that's important to you – purpose and values – this sector might well fit you.   (Andrew West)

This focus on innovation, ideas and delivering value to society is a big part of what makes universities tick. It is evident both in public discourses about the place of universities in wider economic, social and cultural life and within the internal narratives of individual institutions. But precisely how universities should do this has been the subject of much controversy, and this has important implications for what universities are like as places of work – for those in the administration, as well as for the academic staff.

▶ The 'idea' of the university

Before going any further, then, it is worth pausing to consider what universities are and why they exist. This is not as procrastinatory a question as might first appear, because answering it is not straightforward. Quite the contrary, definitions of 'the university' and what universities are for have evolved over time and are evolving still. Indeed, the degree of controversy and passion that accompanies any attempt to define 'the university' or set out its 'purpose' or 'contribution', be that within individual institutions or in wider public discourse, is striking. Taking a little bit of time to understand at least some of what is behind this will help you both in your day-to-day work and in managing your career.

What are universities?
Practically speaking, in many countries including the UK and across much of Europe, the right to use the title of 'university' is restricted to a limited number of institutions that fulfil a specific set of legally defined criteria and is regulated either directly or indirectly by the state. In other countries, such as the USA, a distinction is drawn between those institutions which are accredited through specific agencies approved by the federal government and those which are not, with certain levels of accreditation essential for access to state and/or federal funding. The fact that the state, whether directly or indirectly, commonly has a key role in controlling the use of the term 'university' tells us something important about its value, a value which derives superficially from the power to award degrees but more fundamentally from the power to determine what constitutes legitimate knowledge and to control access to it.

The British definition currently requires a 'university' to:

- have been granted powers to award taught degrees;
- normally have at least 1000 full-time equivalent higher education students, of whom at least 750 are registered on degree courses (including foundation degree programmes), with the number of full-time equivalent higher education students exceeding 55% of the total number of full-time equivalent students; and
- be able to demonstrate that it has regard to the principles of good governance as are relevant to its sector (BIS, 2012).

There is nothing much controversial there, surely? But hidden within those few words are extensive expectations and requirements that have to be fulfilled in order to gain the right to award taught degrees, claim to be delivering *higher*, as opposed to further, education and demonstrate good governance, which includes delivering on all manner of ever-changing government agendas. And this brings us to the key question: what are universities *for*?

What are universities for?

Passionate disputes about what universities are for have been a constant feature of the higher education landscape since the emergence of the modern university in the early nineteenth century. 'Early nineteenth century?', we hear you squeal. 'Surely universities are much older than that?' The answer is, of course, yes and no. Yes, because some of today's most venerable institutions can trace their histories back to the early medieval period, with the term *universitas* first ascribed to a particular group of scholars in Bologna in 1088, before spreading to Paris (founded in about 1150), Oxford (developing by 1167) and beyond over the following 300 years, such that most higher education systems in modern day western Europe can claim to have hosted at least one 'university' before 1500. But no, because these early 'universities' bore only partial resemblance to what would routinely be classed as a university today. Rather, these were scholarly guilds that prepared and licensed young men to enter into a narrow range of professions, primarily, the clergy, the law and, later, medicine. Like other guilds of the time, they were self-regulating, be that as communities of students (Bologna) or 'masters' (Paris, Oxford). However, most were heavily dependent on church and/or royal patronage and were established in their service. Moreover, their focus was on imparting 'revealed' knowledge: notably, much of the intellectual activity that generated the major 'discoveries' of the Renaissance and Enlightenment periods and the emergence of the humanist/scientific tradition took place outside of these institutions (Collini, 2012; Jarvis, 2001).

As such, even though 'universities' are regularly identified – usually with a note of pride – as dominating lists of the oldest surviving institutions of the world, we need to move forward several hundred years to the nineteenth century to find the routine association with 'higher learning' and 'empirical research' that is so fundamental to modern understandings of what distinguishes universities from other post-compulsory educational institutions. This was the height of 'nation-building' across western Europe, with education regarded as critical to national achievement and universities increasingly being ascribed an important role. Several different approaches are identifiable:

- the French (Napoleonic) model of the university, directly controlled by the state and tasked with providing its citizens with the necessary knowledge to be effective upholders of its political unity;
- the Germanic (Humboldtian) model, entrusted by the state to pursue its cultural unity through the scientific pursuit of knowledge within a context of academic freedom in teaching and research; and
- towards the end of that century, the civic universities of the 'new cities' of industrialised England and their equivalents elsewhere, established mainly in the Germanic tradition but with a greater focus on local, as opposed to national, growth and with a particular bent towards science and commerce (or, in the case of the 'land grant' universities in the USA, agriculture).

What these 'new' universities had in common with their medieval ancestors were two things: their role in sharing and – critically – legitimising 'knowledge', albeit through research rather than revelation, and their close reliance on those in power for their own status. Where they differed was in respect of how that knowledge should be generated and shared: through the liberal arts/curiosity-driven model associated with the Humboldtian tradition; or the vocational-technical and applied model of the French approach.

This is not the place for a detailed critique of either approach, both of which are, in any case, ideal types. A vast literature already exists, and some suggested further reading is listed at the end of the chapter. What is important for those seeking to pursue or develop a career in higher education administration is to be aware that this fundamental tension around what universities should be doing persists to this day. Subsequent waves of university foundation, which in the UK context were concentrated in the 1960s, with the incorporation of colleges of advanced technology into the university system, and the 1990s with the abolition of the so-called 'binary line' between self-governing 'chartered' universities and the local government-managed polytechnics (again in favour of 'universities'), did not settle the matter.

More recently, the gradual shift away from 'free' (i.e. publicly funded) undergraduate higher education for individual students in the UK (albeit in divergent ways since devolution) and elsewhere over the last 20 years, the impact of advances in information technology on approaches to the delivery of learning and teaching and the arrival of for-profit higher education providers continue to raise some big questions about what the value of universities is and who gains from it. Similarly, the suggestion that a second 'mode' of knowledge production is emerging, that is much more trans-disciplinary, iterative and grounded in practice has raised questions about where higher education work can and should take place (Nowotny et al., 2003).

How deeply you delve into philosophical debates surrounding the purpose of universities is up to you. But there is little doubt that being aware that they exist will help you to make sense of the changing higher education policy landscape and how different institutions respond. Indeed, many of the contemporary debates about the legitimacy of the notions of research 'impact' and graduate 'employability' and the relationship between universities and wider economic and social well-being that feature strongly in current public policy in the UK and elsewhere continue to turn on this tension:

- Do universities benefit society generally or specifically and what does that mean for how they should be funded and what funders should be able to expect in return?
- Should academic research be undertaken on the basis that it will have an application outside of the academy and has been conceived with that in mind, or because it adds to the general stock of human knowledge and so might, eventually, have an application though perhaps not in our lifetime and possibly in ways of which we cannot yet conceive?
- Is the purpose of higher education teaching to cultivate intellect and scepticism or to prepare the workforce? And should the qualities of 'graduateness' therefore be defined generically or in terms of specific sets of knowledge and skills?
- What should be the relative place of teaching and research within institutional portfolios? Is there a place for 'teaching-only' universities and for the concentration of research activity in a limited group of institutions? Or does that separation detract so fundamentally from the idea of universities as creators of knowledge as to destroy the very idea of a university education itself?

The same can be said of responses to the growth of private providers of higher education (efficient and student-focussed or parasitic asset-strippers) and to the shift from an 'elite' to 'mass' or 'universal' higher education systems in the post-war period (democratising, empowering and raising standards or bureaucratising, de-personalising and compromising standards).

Where the idea of the university goes next is unclear; what is notable perhaps is that successive attempts to 'do universities differently', by making them more applied or more vocational, for example, have faltered. To be sure, it would be difficult to deny that the higher education institutions of today's 'massified' systems, with their much more diverse student bodies, their broad range of funding streams and their extensive teaching and research portfolios, are vastly different from the elite, liberal arts institutions of the early twentieth century. And who knows where the emergence of MOOCs (Massive Open Online Courses) will take us next. However, Collini (2012) has suggested a tendency for universities to revert to type over time. This may account for the endurance of the idea that there should be such a thing as a 'university', in some form, for approaching a thousand years and for the continued influence of Humboldtian ideals despite the shift towards mass higher education and the increasingly skills-based agenda of the knowledge economy.

▶ Universities as workplaces

So, what does this mean for universities as workplaces today? We can answer that question on two levels: practically – in terms of how work is organised formally inside universities; and culturally – in terms of how things are done.

A first thing to note is that universities tend to be big. Given that access to the 'university' title in the UK continues to include a size requirement, this is not surprising. As such, universities are often amongst the largest employers in their local area. Factor in their student populations too and their importance to local economies is significant. With that size comes complexity and specialisation. They are also big in scope – not only in terms of the range of academic disciplines within their portfolio, but also in terms of the diversity of services they provide: not just teaching and research, but also student accommodation, business/enterprise support, galleries and cultural events, sports facilities, healthcare services (mainly for staff and students in the UK, although in the USA this extends to running entire hospitals) and so on. This clearly has implications for the shape of the workforce.

At a most simplistic level, we can categorise university workforces into two main elements: the academics ('faculty' in North American parlance) and 'the rest'. Amongst 'the rest', we find both roles that are recognisable outside of higher education – for example, in finance, human resources, maintenance, marketing and catering – and those that are specific to higher education, such as research management, student support, teaching quality and outreach. We'll look in more detail at this in a few pages' time. But first we need to spend a bit more time understanding how ideas of what universities are for impact upon how universities really work.

The organisational culture of universities

Let's take as a given that there is such a thing as 'organisational culture' and that it can be identified within the rituals, behaviours, stories, terminologies, formal structures and informal power relationships of any organisation (Johnson, 1992, p. 31). Is it possible, then, to speak of a sector-wide 'university culture', that is of certain cultural practices that are common across universities? The literature suggests so, with caveats. On the one hand, we can identify a number of common characteristics of university life that appear to set higher education institutions apart from other types of organisation, many of which apply internationally (Bartell, 2003; Sporn, 1996; Watson, 2013). On the other hand, the extent to which this helps in accounting for behaviour at the level of individual institutions – or, indeed, within different parts of the same institution – at any point in time may be limited (Silver, 2003; Trowler et al., 2012).

Readers already working in university administration may recognise the following common characteristics of universities:

- ambiguous or 'fuzzy' goals that are hard to define and measure, such as advancing knowledge or providing an 'excellent' student experience;
- highly labour-intensive work with abstract outputs (e.g. knowledge, graduates);
- relatively flat hierarchies, combined with a 'loose-coupled' nature, in which individual academic units function with limited reference to each other and great value is placed on academic freedom and autonomy;
- a professionally argumentative nature, combined with a preference for deliberative decision-making and a resistance to management; and
- pronounced differences in primary loyalty between staff categories, with academics often more drawn to their international disciplinary community than to the institution in which they are employed (Becher, 1994; Buckland, 2009; Sporn, 1996; Watson, 2009; Weick, 1976).

These characteristics have several possible implications for the ways in which universities operate. On the one hand, the level of intellectual activity within a university and the fundamental importance attached to the identification, analysis and synthesis of evidence may seem conducive to informed and robust decision-making. On the other, the love of debate, the expectation that anyone can have a view and the absence of an intellectual need to reach a definitive answer can impede decision-making.

For those joining the sector having worked elsewhere, this unwillingness – inability, even – to take decisions quickly, together with an expectation for extensive consultation, can be frustrating. Mark Swindlehurst's experience is typical. He joined Lancaster University as Director of Estates after many years working in the construction industry, latterly as Principal Development Manager for the BBC. Despite familiarity with working through the kind of complex governance structures typical of large publicly funded organisations, he was still surprised by the way in which decisions were made:

> I was questioned about why I fixed the leaking roof in Physics [...], as it was a decision that should have been made by the Estates Committee. And I found that bizarre. I'd been engaged as a professional to spend a maintenance budget to keep the estates operational. I shouldn't need to refer back to the committee to fix a leaking roof!

Add to this a generalised, quasi-ideological resistance to being managed – evident in flat hierarchies, rotational heads of academic units and elaborate committee structures, and summed up within the oft-repeated (and exaggerated?) lament that managing academics is like 'herding cats', which we consider further in Chapter 5 – and we have what we might call an 'interesting' picture.

But it's not all bad by any means. For Sarah Randall-Paley, Director of Finance at Lancaster University, one of the joys of the sector is its collaborative nature:

> My peer group is not that big, there are only about one hundred of us across the UK. We work very collaboratively. We receive delegations from other universities who come to see how we do things here. There is an ethos of learning from each other. I do wonder if that will change though... with private providers coming on the scene.

We'll explore this collaborativeness and its benefits further in Chapter 4 when we look at networking.

That the key 'producers' within universities, that is the academic staff, may have more regard for the 'idea' of the university than the particular institution in which they are employed and more affinity to their international disciplinary peers than their fellow employees is also a challenge, especially if individual disciplines have their own discrete characteristics (Agnew, 2012; Becher, 1994; Trowler et al., 2012). As Hugh Jones, Chief Operating Officer at Cardiff University, observes:

> People's loyalties are with where they got their doctorates. That's where academics get their values and sense of meaning in a discipline. It's no surprise that these translate across universities. [...] It's about habits. I think it's driven by curricula and patterns of work. I think it's inevitable that science and engineering faculties can seem more focused compared to some humanities or social science faculties, because the discipline and what counts as expertise in the discipline is different and people have to work differently to get there. You have to have more contact hours in engineering. I don't think that's because engineers are more hard-working than sociologists. I think it's because you need more time to hear lecturers who are telling you things, whereas in sociology it's more about reading and interpreting it yourself.

Whilst it is important not to make too much of these disciplinary differences or to treat disciplinary cultures as static and fixed, we should also be careful to avoid overstating the extent to which we can speak of a sector-wide culture. Hugh Jones again:

> It's very interesting, the differences where you have universities that are broad – and in my career City University and Cardiff are broad, really multidisciplinary places, versus more specialist institutions – St George's and Goldsmiths. And you can tell the specialist places: they are more harmonious, because you don't have huge differences. But equally, they are more introspective for that same reason, because people don't seem to need to go outside what they are talking about.

David Watson (2000) has pointed to the significance of institutions' historical evolution and 'story-telling' to the way in which they function in the present day. The significance of the pre-/post-1992 distinction (i.e. the old 'binary line') in British higher education, for example, ought not be dismissed: the founding purpose of the polytechnics as vocational and employer-facing and their previous integration into local government structures may make for less commitment to Humboldtian ideals of academic autonomy and a greater acceptance of directive management than is true of the chartered universities (McNay, 1995). Likewise, whether a higher education institution's current shape and size is the result of gradual, internally driven expansion or the consequence of specific crises and/or externally driven mergers may affect how different parts of the institution regard their relationship to the whole, where the formal and informal centres of power lie and what anxieties or enthusiasms drive decision-making. That said, ascribing common cultural traits to institutions on the basis of their past location vis-à-vis the binary line, the timing of their establishment or previous 'bad times' risks over-stating the significance of superficial similarities for the internal life of individual institutions and denies them the capacity to evolve.

In any case, just as it is problematic to talk of a higher education culture per se, so too pinning down the internal culture of a specific higher education institution is difficult. Internal culture is implicit in the way things are done and so may only become apparent when it is offended in some way (Tierney, 1988). Tania Rhodes-Taylor's experiences of culture shock in Case Study 2.1 are a case in point.

Case study 2.1: Tania Rhodes-Taylor, Director of Marketing and Communications, Queen Mary, University of London

Tania Rhodes-Taylor describes her experiences of joining the sector from a corporate culture, thus:

> There seemed to be a kind of code and a mystery around universities that unless you'd always worked in universities, you didn't know what the rules were. You didn't really know how things worked and when you asked people, they got a) very surprised that you asked them and b) suspicious that you asked them. So my first 6–8 months was actually spent in a complete fog because I couldn't figure out one end from the other. I couldn't figure out the jargon, I didn't understand the finance models, I didn't understand why we didn't have things like appraisals and objectives and organisational objectives – all the things that, for me, had been day-to-day.
>
> You'd go into a meeting and Finance would give you a report and, because I was from an environment where you'd been taught to read a profit and loss statement from when you were

> knee high to a grasshopper [...] and all the financial state-
> ments surrounding that, [...I'd] challenge Finance on things
> and there'd be quite a hostile reaction almost. They weren't
> used to that at your level, they were used to their own Finance
> colleagues, it was like 'oh my god, someone's broken into the
> secret cave!' So I found the first six to eight months really
> difficult in terms of trying to figure that out.

The contrast between the corporate and university worlds in
terms of interpersonal relationships was also stark:

> Having come from a commercial organisation where every-
> one was perceived to be of equal value, even if you had
> different roles to perform, the residual difference in perception
> between the value from professional services and academic
> colleagues was – and still is – a bit of a shock. I think it's
> something that's probably changed in the last few years. But
> I was used to talking to Chief Executives of multimillion pound
> organisations on first name terms, so to get shouted out at
> what is a relatively minor meeting by someone who techni-
> cally (if you want to compare it) was more junior than me
> because they didn't like the colour of a font was 'go and lock
> yourself in the loo' time.

Moreover, in complex organisations such as universities, which are
comprised of a range of sub-units with varying degrees of day-to-day
autonomy, the emergence of localised sub-cultures is to be expected
(Kezar and Eckel, 2002; Silver, 2003). Whilst some may replicate or
compliment the dominant culture of the institution as a whole, others
may be at odds with it. Nevertheless, our interviewees all agreed that,
in practical terms recognising and being aware of the potential impact
of organisational culture or cultures within any individual university is
vital for those seeking to succeed in administrative roles.

▶ The 'idea' of higher education administration

Where does all this leave higher education administration? At the risk
of stating the obvious, one thing is certain: universities do not exist to
be administered! And yet here we all are, some 200,000+ of us in the
UK alone according to the Higher Education Statistics Agency's figures

for 2011–2012. Does anyone have an 'idea' of us? Yes, but it ain't all pretty... Behind that figure there lies a tale of shifting roles and power relationships, that according to some is a natural response to the latest evolution of the idea of the university but for others threatens to undermine the very notion of 'the university' itself.

The irresistible rise of the administration?

We noted above that there were approximately 200,000 staff working in the administrative and support roles, broadly defined, within the UK alone in 2011–2012 (HESA, 2013). That equates to some 38% of the total staff population, the remainder being academic staff and technicians. To the extent that universities exist to generate and disseminate knowledge, there is a case to be made that administrative staff should reasonably be classed as overheads, in the sense of being costs incurred over and above those directly associated with an institution's core mission. And the first rule of overheads is: keep them as low as possible. Of course, there is a counter-argument that university responsibilities these days are so complex and multifaceted that many administrative staff have front-line outputs that are as core to mission delivery as those of academic staff. We'll explore that in more detail shortly; for now let's just acknowledge that, whereas universities used to share much of the 'administrative burden' out amongst the academic staff, increasingly that model has become unsustainable, resulting in a shift in staffing profiles in favour of the administration.

The key drivers for this shift have been sector-wide and international and include:

- a shift from an elite to a mass (and thence perhaps to a 'universal' (Trow, 2006)) model of higher education against a backdrop of increasing regulation, resulting in a much larger and more complex student body, the coordination and management of which can no longer be handled effectively by those also tasked with delivering the academic agenda;
- increased pressure on universities to become more 'business-like' by adopting private-sector practices across the board, resulting in greater focus on listening to the needs of customers, growing reputational capital, managing 'talent' and demonstrating value for money, as well as on executive decision-making (Santiago et al., 2006): enter the Student Advisor, the Marketing Manager, the Human Resources Business Partner, the research commercialisation specialist and the policy adviser, as well as – more recently – outsourcing (of catering, student accommodation) and, more recently still, the idea of shared services (often suggested in relation to payroll); and

- reduced but much more directive state funding for higher education, combined with an increased obligation to account for how that funding is used, resulting in new roles and specialisms to deliver and report upon new duties. In the UK, for example, we now have Visa Advisers to help students navigate the rapidly changing world of immigration and Compliance Officers to report back to the government on international students' attendance and completion rates. Staff are also employed to collate annual returns to the Higher Education Statistics Agency and to bring novel research ideas to market.

These changes have also been largely externally imposed. And therein lies the rub: the need for more administration – and more expenditure on overheads – has, to some extent, been forced upon universities, rather than being a conscious decision to invest. At the same time, these administrators, with their own specialist knowledge and expertise, increasingly are engaged in activities that could be interpreted as undermining treasured notions of academic freedom, be that by challenging how academics spend their time (e.g. by suggesting increased student contact hours, improved (as in more) student feedback, or greater engagement with industry) or by sullying the purity of the quest for new knowledge by focussing on short-term returns on investment (e.g. by setting research income targets, questioning the 'viability' of Master's programmes or championing 'income stream diversification').

The 'academic–administrative divide'?
Is this all fine with everyone? Not really. Anyone wanting to get a real insight into where higher education administration sits within universities would do well to spend some time exploring the pages of two very different websites, Times Higher Education, the weekly British 'newspaper' for those working in universities (www.timeshighereducation.co.uk), and the Association of University Administrators, the generic professional body for those working in higher education administration in the UK (www.aua.ac.uk). Of particular note is the contrast between the latter's earnest commitment to 'fostering sound methods of leadership, management and administration' and to 'the advancement of higher education through the robust application of professional knowledge, skills and practices' and the former's critique of 'ever-expanding Human Resources Departments' and revenue-driven curriculum innovations through its spoof 'Poppletonian' newsletter. Its readers' comments on articles that touch upon matters administrative are also eye-opening: indeed, the vitriolic nature of some attacks on those employed in such roles is both fascinating and shocking in equal measure. Just what is this all about?

It's the so-called 'academic–administrative divide', on the rights, wrongs and injustices of which much ink, some tears but hopefully very little blood have been spilled over the years. Whilst it is important not to over-dramatise things or to make lazy generalisations, to deny its existence would be pointless: those already working in universities would scoff, whilst those joining them for the first time would be deceived. Rather, for those seeking to pursue a career in higher education administration, acknowledging its existence and responding appropriately is vital (Conway, 2012; Kuo, 2009).

Seyd summarises the problem thus:

> [A]academics may be characterised by administrators as unworldly, unreliable, incompetent at managerial and administrative tasks, and never in the office when needed to deal with urgent student issues. Administrators, on the other hand, may be viewed by academics as rule-bound, bureaucratic, more concerned with process and systems than with the substance of issues, and lacking in imagination.   (2000, pp. 35–36)

Against this backdrop, it would be all too easy to resort to mutual sniping. But getting involved is not going to help your career progression. Rather, to be successful and fulfilled in your work, it's important to have a sense of what it is that you bring to the table. As Seyd goes on to say, the key thing is to recognise that 'the two groups have different but complementary roles in delivering institutional objectives' and share 'a commitment to excellence and professionalism and to the aims and purposes of higher education' (2000, p. 36).

In one of the first comprehensive examinations of leadership in British universities in the 1990s, Middlehurst observed that administrative roles are primarily concerned with 'the well-being, coordination and regulation of the whole institution: its diverse staff; its range of activities and resources, particularly finance; its extensive plant and equipment' (1993, p. 10). Since then, in the UK context at least, money has become even more complex. Meanwhile, internationally, far more attention is now being paid to 'the student experience', to ensuring academic quality and to engaging with business and with local communities. This is where a good understanding of the nuances of organisational culture within higher education generally and also within individual institutions can make a real difference. As Kuo observed in a study of academic–administrator relationships in a large American public university:

> Depending on the individuals involved and the emerging situations, relationships between academic staff and administrators can

change swiftly. For example, when academic staff and administrators engage in intellectual communication, they tend to be collegial and professional. On the other hand, when communicating about resource allocation, their relationships may become differentiated or fragmentary if they do not agree with each other's perspectives or priorities. [. . . I]n order to achieve collaboration, academic staff and administrators need to attempt to understand how and why their cultural perspectives are similar, different or divided, and what special contexts, situations or challenges affect their interactions. (2009, p. 52)

Good higher education administrators are facilitators. Ultimately, our role is to make sure that our universities function to the very best of their abilities. This can be interpreted in many ways; here are just a few examples:

- helping our universities to understand where talented prospective students can be found and what can be done to encourage them to apply to your university (example role groups: marketing, admissions, access and outreach);
- enabling academic staff to focus on their teaching and research by providing efficient and effective (and non-obtrusive) support (example role groups: course administration, research administration, human resources);
- underpinning the successful functioning of the university by safeguarding its finances and budgeting effectively (example role groups: finance, planning); and
- ensuring that everyone who works or studies in universities has access to high-quality facilities, encompassing everything from a good Wi-Fi connection to well-designed and maintained buildings and well-stocked libraries and more (example role groups: estates, IT support, libraries, maintenance, catering).

In his introduction to *Managing Successful Universities*, renowned higher education expert Michael Shattock explains that, along with good teaching and good research,

good academic support services, good study conditions, a well managed academic and social environment and the ability to take advantage of opportunities as they present themselves all contribute to good learning experiences and to effective education. (2010, p. 1)

This encapsulates not just the purpose of higher education administration, but puts it into the context of the larger machine that is higher education: made up of multiple cogs, the administration works with other gear parts to shape the direction and speed of the university.

Blended roles and the emergence of a 'third space'

At the same time, administrators are increasingly breaking into areas of activity that once were exclusively academic: supporting students, designing novel teaching methods, identifying commercial applications for research outputs and working with potential donors to secure funding (see Case Study 2.2). So much so, in fact, that it's sometimes hard to distinguish where academic roles end and administrative roles begin. This, Celia Whitchurch suggests, has resulted in the emergence of a new category of university worker in the form of the 'blended professional', who occupies a 'third space' that brings together academic and administrator and undertakes 'quasi-academic functions such as conducting study-skill sessions for access students...or conducting overseas recruitment visits' and, in some instances, has 'the possibility of moving into an academic management role, for instance, a pro-vice-chancellor post with a portfolio such as quality, staffing or institutional development' (2008, p. 379). This trend, Whitchurch (2009) notes, is apparent also in the USA and Australia.

Changes in the way academic roles are constructed are also creating new 'opportunities' for administrative staff. Writing of the North American context, Bruce Macfarlane has observed the rise of what he calls the 'para-academic', that is 'individuals who specialise in one element of academic life' (2011, p. 60). Where once an academic would have had responsibility for some teaching, some research and some service elements (e.g. personal tutoring/advising), he argues, such roles are now being unbundled, resulting in the emergence of new job roles that do not require a specifically academic skill-set: delivering student study skills support, project managing large research grants or developing curriculum delivery tools, for example.

The rights and wrongs of this shift aside, it certainly challenges traditional views of whose salaries are direct costs and whose are 'overheads'. It also raises interesting questions about who should take decisions and about what 'academic leadership' really means. The strong view expressed by our interviewees was that universities were and should remain fundamentally academic institutions. The following from Jayne Dowden of Cardiff University is typical:

> The business of a university is to be an academic institution and those at the top need to have a very clear understanding of the

mission of the particular institution – wherever it is in the sector, because we have very different missions – and to be committed to that. So, I'm here not to do great HR [human resources] in its own right; I'm here to deliver HR which is actually appropriate to the vision and mission of the organisation. I can't exist in isolation; I have to make what I do serve that greater purpose. I think when you have people who can't understand that and who see their role as actually existing almost in its own right, then you get into difficulties.

Hugh Jones, also from Cardiff, goes further:

If you want to be in charge of an organisation, you should not become a university administrator. Fundamentally academic leadership is at the heart of being a university. There's a strand of thinking that says you shouldn't rule out administrators from becoming university leaders, and although in terms of individual skills, I don't doubt there are people who could do it, I do think that culturally it would be a very, very bad thing and I think that it would distract universities from what they are doing.

[…] Which is not to equate university administration with a forelock tugging deference. It's not like that at all. But it is recognising that this is a partnership deal. I think one of the ways that one can be a successful administrator is: remember to make yourself useful and that way no one asks the question called 'why are we paying you anyway', which is always a worry! But there is something, which is that, when push comes to shove, academic communities think they are in charge. And in lots of ways, they ought to be.

We'll explore in more detail some of the practical challenges this presents for those in administrative roles in Chapter 5, when we look at 'management'. For now, it's important to note that this does not mean that senior administrative staff should not be involved in leading universities, nor that their leadership contributions should be delivered covertly. On the contrary, it would be unusual these days to find university senior management team meetings that did not include – and value – some 'non-academic' representation. Indeed, though it remains unusual in the UK, in both North America and Australia it is not uncommon to find the senior administrative post-holder in the institution accorded the title of Vice-President or Deputy Vice Chancellor with an appropriate suffix (e.g. Resources; Administration and Finance; Corporate), without having followed an academic career path. The challenge is to remain grounded in what Jon Baldwin, Deputy Vice Chancellor for

Professional Services of Murdoch University in Australia, describes as 'the academic rhythms of the institution' and, he goes on, 'to know your place. I think that's just good common sense. You'll get the best from relationships if you engage in them and if they are mutually respectful, whatever your relative power'.

Case study 2.2: Liesl Elder, Director of Development, University of Oxford

Liesl Elder, Director of Development at the University of Oxford, is sanguine about the realities of the so-called academic–administrative divide:

> When I was working for the University of Durham, the old building we worked in was called the Old Shire Hall and the rest of university used to call it 'the Kremlin', where the evil administration lived. I do feel that sometimes when I walk into a room, the Darth Vader theme music ought to be playing!

> But that's part of just the community of universities, the give and take of the academics versus the staff, administration versus the academic pursuit. That's true of every university I've worked at, I think it's part of the milieu that we work in. I've never been bothered by it, I just think it's one of those things that is the common language of our community. If you get hung up on the fact that the administration is not well-liked then probably university administration is not for you.

But her message is not one of 'put up or shut up':

> We [the fundraising operation] have to prove that we're valuable, so I spend a lot of time talking to people about what the office does, being frank about our shortcomings as well as the sorts of things we do that are successful and I think that buys credibility. I think if we can admit that we are not good at everything, on the one hand it's exposing weakness, on the other hand it shows we're addressing problems, recognising problems.

> [...A]ll the senior people we work with just have to have frank conversations about what works and what doesn't work. As long as they understand that ultimately we want to help

them achieve their goals, that's why we're here – to be a facilitating factor in a university being more successful. And I want to know if things aren't working. If it's not working, then let's fix it. I'm very transparent about that but apparently that's unusual!

I really see us as a service department even though fundraisers tend to be quite external and lots of folk think of them as the sales arm. Ultimately you have to have a very firm connection with the people you're working for because ultimately we're an extension of the academics, we're facilitating their activity, so [we need to be] tuned in.

▶ Towards a higher education administration 'profession'?

The trend towards increased specialisation of roles within university administration is reflective of what has been happening in society more generally. In the knowledge-based economy, the ability to demonstrate 'expertise' has become increasingly important as a means of distinguishing ourselves from other knowledge workers and this has implications for the organisation of work. One facet of this has been an observable increase in the number of job roles now described as 'professions' – for example, in engineering, accountancy, nursing, human resources, information technology, project management, counselling, coaching and so on (see Chapter 6).

What can legitimately be described as a 'profession' is a matter of debate, but commonly identified traits include:

- the identification of a particular body of knowledge shared by members and with which they are expected to remain engaged;
- barriers to entry, typically in the form of (higher-level) qualifications or licencing;
- agreed standards of practice, underpinned by a shared code of ethics; and
- a system of self-regulation, including the capacity to sanction, discipline or expel members.

The appeal of being regarded as a profession comes in part from the authority that it confers. And it is notable that universities have played a significant role in supporting this trend, gradually drawing in an increasing number of fields of expertise into their sphere of influence over the course of the twentieth century, most recently in the allied health professions, with others knocking at the door in their quest for legitimation (Grimley, 2013; Moyes, 2013).

But what of higher education administration itself? We noted earlier the existence of a 'professional body' for higher education administrators in the UK and equivalent bodies exist across the sector internationally. But so too do a growing number of specialist bodies covering a wide range of activities, some focussed on areas that are unique to higher education (student services, schools liaison, research administration), others adding a further level of specialism to areas of expertise that are more portable between sectors (finance, estate management, marketing, human resources, information technology). The benefits of engaging with such groups are explored further in the following two chapters. Certainly, these bodies support the view of a move to 'professionalise' higher education administration in the sense of identifying common knowledge and behaviour frameworks, but does that mean that we can speak of a 'higher education profession' within universities existing in parallel to the academic profession? And would such a thing even be desirable?

The jury is still out (Szekeres, 2011). On the one hand, you may encounter those who dismiss the notion of a higher education profession as a poorly disguised attempt to justify the bureaucratisation of university life by ascribing to a disparate body of pen-pushers a nobility and honour they simply do not deserve (see Times Higher Education's readers' comments, *passim!*). Less dramatically, there is concern that the growth of specialist roles within higher education may create professional 'silos' which are career-limiting for individuals (Shine, 2010) and also hinder the capacity of the administration truly to support the institution (Andrews, 2013). In the same way as specialisation in academic roles has paved the way for administrative staff to infiltrate previously inaccessible areas of university work, so too has specialisation within the administration opened up universities to functional experts from other fields, with an observable trend towards recruiting to senior posts from outside the sector in recent years (Shine, 2010). Good news if you want to move across into the university sector; less so if you want to progress within it, perhaps?

On the other hand, the absence of a professional framework in the context of a knowledge-based economy is a concern. As one experienced higher education administrator, who has also worked in government and in the private sector, told us:

> In universities, the balance has been very strongly on the side of academics running the place and administration being seen as

something lower graded, lower status, less important, not valuable, not needed, a barrier getting in the way telling them what to do: and that's all the things it shouldn't be doing. That's actually militated against administration being seen in its own right as something that should have a standard and should have levels of quality and careers and career paths and a journey for the people who are in there as compared with other sectors.   (Kirsten Gillingham)

This may be where the value of the idea of higher education administration as a profession comes to the fore: by suggesting that there is a body of knowledge and a set of common standards that those engaged in the business of supporting universities should share, regardless of their particular specialist expertise. As Matthew Andrews, Chair of the UK's Association of University Administrators, 2012–2014, puts it:

To be effective requires a good knowledge of why the role exists, how it fits in to the broader higher education landscape, and what the pressures and trends are within the sector more broadly; in other specialisations and for staff working in more senior or more junior positions. To work in the silo alone is to fail to be as effective as our institutions need us to be.   (2013, p. 3)

Perhaps, then, the value of having an 'idea' of higher education administration may be its capacity to root such staff in the idea of the 'university' itself?

▶ Conclusion

Universities are fascinating places to work: their history, their culture and the expectations placed upon them combine to create an environment in which those who are service-orientated can flourish. However, careers in university administration are not for the faint-hearted: it takes a certain kind of resilience and creativity to be effective in a context in which a (small) proportion of your colleagues think that your very existence heralds the end of days and are not afraid to tell you so, or alternatively, are polite to your face but in their every deed undermine all your hard work. But there is also great joy to be had from being part of a sector that is, fundamentally and however conceived, driven by a desire to challenge existing assumptions and make things better. As we have discussed in this chapter, appreciating what is really at stake, what drives universities and what that means for how you understand your contribution as part of the administration is critical. In the following chapter, we explore some of the practical steps you can take to equip yourself to be effective in that environment.

▶ Further reading

Bok, D. C. (2013) *Higher Education in America*, Oxford: Princeton University Press.

Callender, C. and Scott, P. (2013) *Browne and Beyond: Modernizing English Higher Education*, London: Institute of Education Press.

Garrett, G. and Davies, G. (2010) *Herding Cats: Being Advice to Aspiring Academic and Research Leaders*, Axminster: Triarchy Press.

Handy, C. (1999) *Understanding Organizations*, London: Penguin.

McGettigan, A. (2013) *The Great University Gamble: Money, Markets and the Future of Higher Education*, London: Pluto.

Shattock, M. (2012) *Making Policy in British Higher Education: 1945–2011*, Maidenhead: Open University Press.

Washburn, J. (2005) *University Inc: The Corporate Corruption of Higher Education*, New York: Basic Books.

▶ References

Agnew, M. (2012) 'Strategic planning: An examination of the role of disciplines in sustaining internationalization of the university', *Journal of Studies in International Education*, 17(2), 183–202.

Andrews, M. (2013) 'What is an administrator?' *Newslink*, 77, 3–4.

Bartell, M. (2003) 'Internationalization of universities: A university culture-based framework', *Higher Education*, 45(1), 43–70.

Becher, T. (1994) 'The significance of disciplinary differences', *Studies in Higher Education*, 19(2), 151–161.

BIS (2012) Ten institutions on track to become universities, https://www.gov.uk/government/news/ten-institutions-on-track-to-become-universities, accessed 27 June 2013.

Buckland, R. (2009) 'Private and public sector models for strategies in universities', *British Journal of Management*, 20(4), 524–536.

Collini, S. (2012) *What Are Universities For*? London: Penguin.

Conway, M. (2012) 'Using Causal Layered Analysis to explore the relationship between academics and administrators in universities', *Journal of Future Studies*, 17(2), 37–58.

Grimley, B. (2013) *Theory and Practice of NLP Coaching: A Psychological Approach*, London: Sage.

HESA (17 January 2013) Staff at Higher Education Institutions in the UK 2011/12 (SFR 1850), http://www.hesa.ac.uk/index.php?option=com_content&task=view&id=2662&Itemid=161, accessed 25 November 2013.

Jarvis, P. (2001) *Universities and Corporate Universities*, London: Kogan Page.

Johnson, G. (1992) 'Managing strategic change – strategy, culture and action', *Long Range Planning*, 25(1), 28–36.

Kezar, A. and Eckel, P. D. (2002) 'The effect of institutional culture on change strategies in higher education – Universal principles or culturally responsive concepts?' *Journal of Higher Education*, 73(4), 435–460.

Kuo, H.-M. (2009) 'Understanding relationships between academic staff and administrators: An organisational culture perspective', *Journal of Higher Education Policy and Management*, 31(1), 43–54.

Macfarlane, B. (January 2011) 'The morphing of academic practice: Unbundling and the rise of the para-academic', *Higher Education Quarterly*, 65(1), 59–73.

McNay, I. (1995) 'From the collegial academy to corporate enterprise: The changing cultures of universities', in Schuller, T. (ed.), *The Changing University?* Buckingham: SRHE/Open University Press, 105–115.

Middlehurst, R. (1993) *Leading Academics*, Buckingham: SRHE & Open University Press.

Moyes, H. (2013) 'Book review: Theory and practice of NLP coaching', *Perspectives: Policy and Practice in Higher Education*, published online 14 August 2013.

Nowotny, H., Scott, P. and Gibbons, M. (2003) 'Introduction: "Mode 2" revisited: The new production of knowledge', *Minerva*, 41, 179–194.

Santiago, R., Carvalho, T., Amaral, A. and Meek, V. L. (2006) 'Changing patterns in the middle management of higher education institutions: The case of Portugal', *Higher Education*, 52(2), 215–250.

Seyd, R. (2000) 'Breaking down barriers: The administrator and the academic', *Perspectives: Policy and Practice in Higher Education*, 4(2), 35–37.

Shattock, M. (2010) *Managing Successful Universities*, Maidenhead: Open University Press.

Shine, J. (2010) *Professional Careers in Higher Education: Institutional Perspectives*, London: Leadership Foundation for Higher Education.

Silver, H. (2003) 'Does a university have a culture?' *Studies in Higher Education*, 28(2), 157–169.

Sporn, B. (1996) 'Managing university culture: An analysis of the relationship between institutional culture and management approaches', *Higher Education*, 32(1), 41–61.

Szekeres, J. (2011) 'Professional staff carve out a new space', *Journal of Higher Education Policy and Management*, 33(6), 679–691.

Tierney, W. G. (1988) 'Organizational culture in higher-education – defining the essentials', *Journal of Higher Education*, 59(1), 2–21.

Trow, M. (2006) 'Reflections on the transition from elite to mass to universal access: Forms and phases of higher education in modern societies since WWII', in Altbach, P. and Forest, J. (eds), *International Handbook of Higher Education*, Volume 18, Dordrecht: Springer, 243–280.

Trowler, P., Saunders, M. and Bamber, V. (eds) (2012) *Tribes and Territories in the 21st Century: Rethinking the Significance of Disciplines in Higher Education*, Abingdon: Routledge.

Watson, D. (2000) *Managing Strategy*, Buckingham: Open University Press.

Watson, D. (2009) *The Question of Morale. Managing Happiness and Unhappiness in University Life*, Maidenhead: Open University Press.

Watson, D. (2013) *The Question of Conscience: Higher Education and Personal Responsibility*, London: Institute of Education Press.

Weick, K. (1976) 'Educational organizations as loosely coupled systems', *Administrative Science Quarterly*, 21, 1–19.

Whitchurch, C. (2008) 'Shifting identities and blurring boundaries: The emergence of third space professionals in UK higher education', *Higher Education Quarterly*, 62(4), 377–396.

Whitchurch, C. (2009) 'The rise of the "Blended Professional" in higher education: A comparison between the United Kingdom, Australia and the United States', *Higher Education*, 58, 407–418.

3 Knowing How to Develop Your Skills and Experience

▶ Introduction

So, we've explored what it's like to work in universities; this chapter is about 'what you know', about the practical side managing your career. It's about what you can do to enhance your 'toolbox' of skills and knowledge to deploy in new situations. The main messages that we want to convey throughout this book are that working in higher education is an interesting and rewarding career choice, and that, if you want it to be your career, then you need to start to manage it as early as possible.

Amanda Wilcox, Senior Advisor, Pro-Vice-Chancellors' Office, University of Hull, has this to say about working in higher education:

> [HE is] a profession that is crying out for well-qualified, intelligent individuals. It is a very rewarding career with lots of opportunities for people to make a difference and to progress both within and between institutions. The administrative and professional services are always looking for individuals who have strong people and transferable skills, and who are motivated by problem solving. The effective, efficient and innovative management of universities is becoming increasingly important and we need good people to do it.

Let's start with a question – what do we mean by career success? This has as many different answers as there are people you could ask, but research tells us that it can be broken down into two major components: extrinsic success, such as increased salary, and intrinsic success, such as someone's own satisfaction with their job.

Many staff (and especially women) report intrinsic rewards as their main motivation, and this could be expected in higher education – see also Chapter 2 for more on the reasons that people choose to work in universities. Research by Gander (2010) with middle-management women administrators supports the idea that intrinsic rewards are the most important for this group with comments such as: 'I'm never going to take a job again because it is the "right" thing to do', 'what is important and motivating to me...is to do something that interests me' and '...at what grade is not important'. These sentiments are likely to be as relevant for men as they are for women and they give us a further flavour of why people want to work in higher education. Indeed, as Jon Baldwin, Deputy Vice Chancellor (Professional Services), Murdoch University says:

> If someone looks at my career they might think that it was planned, but [it was] nothing of the sort really. If you work hard and if you take advantage of all the opportunities around you to develop in your own job, then the next job just kind of finds you as much as you finding it.

However, as much as we love our current roles, we spend a long time at work and inevitably we are going to want to move around, develop ourselves, contribute something to our organisations and maybe see what we can achieve. Recent research (Converse et al., 2012) indicates that having a proactive personality was a predictor of extrinsic career success. Some of this was because both proactive personalities and those that had higher self-control achieved higher educational results, automatically leading to jobs with higher extrinsic rewards. However, individuals with higher self-control also seemed to be more willing and able to manage greater work-related responsibilities. This would lead us to assume that most administrative staff fall into this category (high educational attainment and ergo high self-control), which means that we should be able to take on more work-related projects to help us to achieve our extrinsic success.

Intrinsic success is as, if not more, important. Many of us have been unlucky enough to be in jobs that we haven't particularly liked and know just how de-motivating this can be; salary perhaps could be said to be more of a hygiene factor than a motivating one for us (using Herzberg's theory of motivation). So then, if we are capable of achieving work-related success how do we go about maximising our opportunities? Burke and Attridge (2011) interviewed 101 people in the USA earning at least $100,000 in a variety of occupations. The themes that emerged from this research that the participants thought contributed most to their success were having had opportunities to develop managerial and interpersonal skills. Additionally, positive types of work experience that they thought contributed included general management skills, having challenging work assignments or positions, development of operational and business line management skills,

Figure 3.1 Different aspects to manage within your career

having a diverse range of work positions, networking, being politically savvy about interpersonal communication, having a good boss and mentor and completing professional training. Many of these themes are important in higher education as well and are covered below; Figure 3.1 shows different aspects that we may wish to reflect on when planning our career development.

▷ Qualifications

Qualifications are important for us in higher education for two reasons. Firstly, we work in a knowledge-based sector and to understand and work with our academic colleagues we have to be grounded in their world. Secondly, qualifications are seen as proxies for competence. How much do you really use the knowledge gained from your first or second (or third or fourth) degrees in your day job – not much I bet. It could be argued that knowledge from, for example, an MBA or technical skills training is used more often, but still perhaps not really that much. What about a PhD – might this lend instant credibility, putting us on par with our academic colleagues? Perhaps, but this is not a reason enough to pursue a PhD. At the end of the day, we've chosen to be in roles that aren't academic – and we should see that as a positive career choice. What it does tell people is that we have the level of intellectual ability to have 'collected' these qualifications and a level of analytical and critical thinking skills that can be applied to new situations. This is particularly important for women and other under-represented staff: research shows that generally these groups have a higher level of educational attainment than men in similar roles as it can be used as a compensating factor against discrimination (Doherty and Manfredi, 2009; Singh et al., 2008). One colleague we spoke to even said that 'I felt that if I wanted to progress I wasn't going to get there on my own merit, I needed to have something that would prove that I could be promoted...so that was my motivation for doing an MBA'.

In our sector then, getting your qualifications in order is probably one of the simplest and most immediate tasks that you can take to start managing your career. If you aspire to being promoted to the graduate administrator posts, then getting a degree is necessary. Although person specifications for job vacancies often say that you can have 'equivalent experience', we say why take the risk? However, this can be a big leap (although you could take a Certificate or Diploma in Higher Education first). Another good way of gaining a qualification in the UK is to study for the Postgraduate Certificate in Professional Practice run by the Association of University Administrators (AUA). The aim of this course is to use your understanding of higher education as a practitioner and to develop further your critical reflection of professional practice and awareness of developments within the sector.

If you have recently graduated, you can enter higher education via a graduate trainee scheme. These offer an excellent opportunity and can be invaluable in setting you up for a career in university administration. They are however fiercely competitive with, it's been reported, up to 150 or so applications for one intake, so you really need to have something to make you stand out from the crowd. In the UK, the Association of Heads of University Administration launched a graduate programme in 2012 for university leadership called Ambitious Futures. The programme selects graduates from participating higher education institutions to spend two placements at their home university and one at another university. The benefit of these schemes is that the successful candidates build up experience in a very short period of time.

For example, a similar scheme that runs at the University of Nottingham places people in four placements of three months each in a 12-month period. So, in 12 months you gain knowledge and experience of four different areas of the institution. Of course, institutions don't guarantee jobs at the end of the scheme; but with the amount of knowledge and skills accumulated in that time, as well as being able to prove being able to adapt to change, the likelihood of gaining permanent employment at a university after this is extremely high. As Paul Greatrix, Registrar of Nottingham University, says of Nottingham's scheme:

> [This] would be fantastic because it would provide a consistent base for growing the profession of higher education administration, and also giving new administrators the opportunity to see a

broad range and identify where they want to make their next move and give them a broader overview than they'd otherwise get. You get four to eight years of experience compressed into one year or 18 months and it's really positive and you learn an awful lot from it. I'm just really excited because I think it's the thing I would have loved to have done when I started all those years ago. Otherwise you have to apply for jobs or you have to move around or wait for someone else to move you in order for it to happen.

If you already have some level of qualification, are working in administration and want to be promoted to a more senior role, you could get a postgraduate qualification. In the UK, there are only a few specific postgraduate qualifications you can take such as the MBA (Higher Education Management) from the Institute of Education, the MSc in Education (Higher Education) from the University of Oxford or the MA in International Higher Education from the University of Nottingham.

In the USA, this is a far more developed field with a number of institutions offering Masters qualifications; for example, Stanford University offers an MBA (Higher Education), Harvard University offers a Master of Education (Higher Education) and Northwestern University offers a MSc in Higher Education Administration and Policy, to name but a few. In Australia, Macquarie University offer a Master of Higher Education, and the University of Sydney offers an MEd in Educational Management and Leadership.

Although in the UK senior job roles are not yet asking for specific qualifications, many do ask for evidence of continuing professional development, such as an appropriate professional qualification. With the growth in administration specialists and increased emphasis on running universities as 'businesses', or at least in a more 'business-like fashion', one may expect these types of qualification to become a requirement in the not too distant future. If you're a woman or from another under-represented group, as mentioned above, the literature suggests this may be even more important.

As we work with academic colleagues and/or in research administration, we'd also recommend getting some sort of research experience under your belt. This doesn't have to be a full blown PhD/EdD: it could be a research methodology course or a Master's with a dissertation. You could do a small institutional project and write it up for publication in a professional journal such as the AUA's *Perspectives: Policy and Practice in Higher Education*, which will give you an understanding of what academics have to go through as part of the writing and publishing process. In any case, undertaking these types of activities not only makes us better administrators, but also helps raise the standard of administration across the board.

Think about where you're going to get your qualifications from. If it's your first degree and your institution will pay for it as part of your benefits scheme, then that would be the most obvious choice. If you're looking at a higher level qualification such as a Master's, think about what you want to get out of it before making your final decision. Obviously your institution may have a Master's course that you will be able to take. If not, there are two basic options. Do you want a generic qualification from a good school (MBAs can be triple accredited[1]) to give you a different insight into business, a different network and to keep your career options open? If you know you're going to work in higher education for your whole or majority of your career, then maybe you want a more specific course that focusses on university management. This is certainly the route the three authors took: we all knew our careers were in higher education, and our programme would enable us to network with colleagues at various higher education institutions, as well as to think about 'business' from a higher education perspective and to enhance our understanding of the differences and similarities between universities and commercial organisations.

▶ Continuing professional development

Continuing professional development (CPD) can be very useful for giving you short, intense training and development on a whole plethora of subjects. What is appropriate CPD for you is going to depend on both your institution and your role. Look at Case Study 3.1 for an example that shows the usefulness of specific skills and knowledge development courses. Tracey Carlton shows that you don't necessarily need to be a subject expert at the start of your career as long as you've got the right set of soft skills to work with people and the right approach and behaviours. You can learn the specifics of the role using the right CPD courses.

> ### Case study 3.1: Tracey Carlton: Head of Product and Service Development, Marketing Unit, The Open University
>
> After I had finished my PhD I got a role on a fixed-term contract as a Project Manager in the Science Faculty for six months at The Open University working on a human brain CD-ROM. At about the time of the CD being completed, the Faculty was looking to appoint a permanent Marketing Manager at a G7 [Spinal point

30–36]. Although I didn't have any experience I wanted a permanent role and for some reason they gave me the job. For the first few years I was up-skilling learning about marketing – that was how I fell into marketing. I trained in marketing by taking the two year corporate route through the Chartered Institute of Marketing and then later on I did some Ashridge [Business School] courses on strategy and leadership which complement the marketing knowledge. After some time in the Faculty I was re-graded to a G8 [Spinal point 37–43] and I was doing lots of different things in this role such as writing business cases, associated research and communications – the whole end to end process.

The University then took the decision to centralise all the marketing managers into the Marketing Unit and I had to re-apply for my role. I applied for several of the available roles and I was successful in gaining a G9 [Spinal point 45–50] as Head of Product Marketing. I had limited experience of products and partnerships so I spent some time on these type of courses to get a foundation. After another restructure my role was expanded and regraded to a G10 [senior salary band], which is the role I do currently.

I'd say that my experience shows that if you have the right behaviours and approach to work you can gain the specific knowledge and skills but it is far harder to train someone if they need to improve their soft skills. I really enjoy working here because it's been fulfilling as I have created my roles and have been able to create new things, for example the first CD-ROM to be published and the first module leaflets to be published, amongst various other things. It is the fact that I could bring things in that made a real difference to this university that made it enjoyable, and also that the fact that people respect me for the job I do. That's very important to me and that fact that I have integrity and the reputation that I hold here.

CPD courses can be broken down into two themes: skills and knowledge based development and leadership and personal development.

Skills and knowledge-based development

Skills development courses are very important at the beginning to mid-career stages. At the start of your career, you need to be performing excellently in your role (we can't reiterate this strongly enough, and the following sections will help you understand how to be a reflective practitioner) and to be seen to add value to the projects and activities you take on. Skills development CPD therefore really helps you consolidate your current knowledge and learn new practices and techniques. A balance between skills to enhance your current role and skills to develop your career are ideal.

For example, if you have some project-management-type responsibility, you might benefit from taking a Prince2 project management course to learn methodologies that can be adapted easily to the higher education environment and give you a set of skills that can add value to managing your projects. If you want to get your first line management role, then take some in-house courses such as managing performance. We are lucky working in higher education institutions as the human resources or staff development departments normally have extensive CPD offerings tailored around the core competencies that have been identified by the institution as central to particular roles. For mid- to senior-level staff, more high-level skills development is useful, such as, for example, change management or gaining Chartered status, dependent on your career aspirations.

Kirsten Gillingham, Bursar at St Antony's College, Oxford has this to say about skills development:

> To me, the core of good skills development actually does hinge around performance review because that gives a framework for having a good conversation about how we're going to develop skills and recognising that there are skills to develop and it's a good thing to be doing... In other settings, I've seen training programmes far more structured and developed than that and I saw that whole notion of developing a whole core of skill sets at the University of London. I saw it at Brighton [University] and some of those were hinged around the core competencies in the management standards: actually building up and beginning to relate jobs to where the skill sets are against management standards and then looking for tailored provision for a whole organisation. On a big scale, you can do that for a whole university, a tailored training set of modules that people can work through at their own pace as they need.

Knowledge-based courses are important at all stages of your career as they provide specialist knowledge to allow you become more informed in aspects of the job you are currently carrying out. Examples of this type of CPD are learning about intellectual property, risk management, employment law and strategy, all to help you in carrying out specific activities, or more general courses such as mentoring, coaching or understanding equality and diversity. Kirsten Gillingham again:

[...] interestingly [my own skills development is] something that I haven't concentrated on recently and I'm conscious I need to [...]. The fact that I could be in this job for another ten years (what a thought) [means that] it's really important that I keep developing. I've had to develop just to pick up the job and learn, so there's been a lot of learning involved in just doing the job, but once I get familiar with all the angles of the job, I need then to push myself to learn more and deepen or broaden consciously my skill set. Either through some sort of formal training or just pushing my own research really and feeling that I'm understanding it as fully as I can, and really pushing boundaries. The moment you get complacent in a job is the point you stop learning or trying or think you can do it is the start of getting incompetent.

Leadership and personal development

Leadership and personal development courses are important throughout your career but arguably become more important the more senior you become. The AUA has as one of their competencies 'managing self and personal skills', which encompasses being 'willing and able to assess... [your] own skills, abilities and experience [and] being aware of [your] own behaviour and how it impacts on others'. Many other professional organisations will have some form of this reflective behaviour as a key competence, as do higher education institutions' own competency frameworks. A good way of starting to reflect on your practice is to undertake a 360 degree feedback process. These come in various forms but usually require your line manager, staff and colleagues to rate your competence on a number of factors, depending on what process you're undertaking.

In the UK, leadership courses range from those in first line management positions such the Institute of Leadership and Management's *Team Leading* certificate through to the *Top Management Programme* run by the Leadership Foundation for Higher Education. The LH Martin Institute provides similar opportunities for those working in tertiary education in Australia and New Zealand. If you ask people who are already at the top in their chosen areas in higher education institutions, nearly all of them will say that being a reflective practitioner, or indeed a reflexive practitioner, is the key to being successful. Tessa Harrison, Registrar at Southampton University says this about her CPD:

> I'm quite an organised person and I'm somebody who, I'd say for the last fifteen years easily, has always been very actively reflecting. I've always done an end of term review, obviously always taken appraisal very seriously and always had a plan for improving

myself. So CPD has been really important and I've always mixed the finding out bit and going on courses bit because I've wanted to find out about something, with the skills development piece. I've always been very conscious of where my skills are and where they need to be and making sure that I'm actively working on that. I will only go on things when I've identified I need some skills development. A good example is when I was at the University of the West of England and they asked me to become the clerk to governors. That was a whole new area I just had no idea about at all, I knew about Senate, but I had no idea about corporate governance at all, so I thought okay, I've just got to learn some stuff and I signed up for the Leadership Foundation's introduction course for clerks and secretaries.

Being able to review your actions and/or behaviours and change them as required – and, indeed, to think critically about the impact of your own assumptions, biases, values and actions as you work – will help you develop as a manager and leader and is critically important.

CPD, then, is not just about formal learning. Reading books and articles, thinking critically about the wider context and talking and listening to others can also be really important. As Jon Baldwin says:

I think you've got to devour the material that's around you, you've got to read things like the *Times Higher*, you've got to read things like *The Guardian*, you've got to pick up the odd book and delve into it in terms of what people think about HE management and administration. You've got to make your work a bit of your hobby; not your life, but a bit of your hobby as well [...] going to those professorial lectures than you can go to, going to receptions about this and that and the other, listening to what your VC and other senior colleagues say, thinking about it.

▶ Personal development plan

There is, as suggested above, an extensive array of CPD courses that could be undertaken both at your own institution and through external providers. In fact, you could spend most of your time on a course, but we don't recommend that! A really good way of thinking with clarity about what activities you should be spending your time doing is by developing a personal development plan (PDP). There are many templates for doing this; one example that is freely available is on the AUA website (AUA, 2013). Spending some time thinking analytically about your current development needs is invaluable. This could be based on a 360 feedback process, new activities that you'll be undertaking in the coming year, or feedback from your line manager.

Tania Rhodes-Taylor, Director of Marketing and Communications at Queen Mary University of London, has ensured that

> everybody in the department has a development plan, everybody has training as part of that and everybody has an objective that's related to their next step. It's not development just to do with their current job, it's [also] development to do with the next job so everybody has a stretch objective that's related to the next job they want to do. We talk about what's the next job that you want to do at appraisal – where do you want to go next, what do we do to facilitate that. So I've built that into the process and now it's just part of standard process.

This is where your reflective practice comes in. It is vitally important to be able to reflect on your skills and behaviours, accept constructive criticism and feedback and react logically rather than just emotionally (although, of course, we're all prone to reacting emotionally first). We have almost certainly all met colleagues whose view of themselves and their abilities is at odds with their reputation, which means they probably have never been able to reflect and marry up feedback with their own views of their strengths and weaknesses. Reflective practice then can lead us away from some more negative traits to more positive ones, allowing us to become more open:

- Instead of being self-absorbed, we convey humility.
- Instead of feeling out of depth, we feel open to learn.
- Instead of feeling out of context, we become open to experience.   (Raelin, 2002)

A good way of starting your reflective practice is to try and understand yourself better and be able to understand the viewpoint of your colleagues. There are many tools for this but one that is based on sound academic research over more than half a century, and has shown to be useful especially in understanding others, is the Myers–Briggs Indicator Type (The Myers & Briggs Foundation, 2013). This uses specific questioning to categorise individuals into 16 distinctive personality types. Myers–Briggs say that it 'can help you with career planning at every stage: from your choices of subjects in school to choosing your first career, to advancing in your organisation or changing careers later in life'. If you start to look into this and take the test yourself, it will possibly be surprising how accurate it is, even if we all think we're individuals and couldn't possibly be categorised in this way.

You can also think about your one- to two-year (or longer) plan – what do you want your next role to be, how will you get there, what skills do you need to achieve this? What skills and knowledge are required in person specifications of advertised jobs? Your institution may have competencies based around themes that they think are key; the AUA also has competencies. Use these frameworks as part of your analysis – where are the gaps in your skills?

Case Study 3.2 shows a Vice Chancellor's view of the use of competencies to enhance career progression. Making this part of your annual appraisal in discussion with your line manager will keep you on track. Feedback given to a colleague of one of the authors who was being mentored by a senior manager surprised her, as she was asked what her five-year plan was. She didn't have one, and she couldn't see past her next objective. Additionally, the senior manager asked her what her next plan was, once she'd achieved the objective on her current plan – so don't just stop once you've achieved your next objective, continue to plan and set objectives.

Case study 3.2: Martin Bean, Vice Chancellor, The Open University

Career progression I think has to be grounded in competencies and pathways, and I don't believe it's any more complicated in the administrative side of the institution than the academic side. I think the good thing in the administrative side of the university is that competencies can be somewhat more generic across the different disciplines so there's more ability to transfer between various areas. However, I do think for any university to be successful at building career pathways in the administration it does need to be clear about these disciplines and competencies. Think of it as the vertical and horizontal – what are the competencies that are discreet for a particular discipline and what are the competencies that are horizontal, that run across disciplines? Then think what are the main disciplines? You'll have people of course that are more general in nature and you'll have people that are more discipline specific. If you took IT as an example, you're more likely to have people who are more discipline-centric and who you wouldn't be able to easily pick up and put somewhere else, whereas if you take people in the Secretary's Office they are probably building a set of competencies that can be just as valuable picked up and put in Estates as they would be in Human Resources as they would be in some other area.

I think what we should focus on is what human beings like – we like blueprints so when you're discussing careers it can't just be abstract, we all like structure, we like to say 'well I'm at this level and these are the things that I want to do, so now let me look at the blueprint'. This is when the competencies kick in because then you can look at a list of competencies that someone in that role would need and then you can do a gap analysis between the person's current competencies and the competencies for the next job.

In the perfect world the institution's training and development would kick in and a lot of organisations do that really well, often backed up by great technology that helps. Certainly at the companies that I've come from in the private sector that is how it would work so what you've got then is a really structured way of saying 'right, my boss thinks I'm good on all of these but I need to develop in these areas'. I'm looking at how I view myself and thinking 'oh there are some blind spots, I didn't know that, and there's some confirming evidence so let's go with the confirming evidence and discuss the blind spots'.

▶ Gaining experience

Apart from your qualifications and CPD, you need to add some actual hard work experience to maximise your career opportunities. Indeed, in the research cited above, Burke and Attridge (2011) identified opportunities to have challenging work assignments and a diverse range of experience as a key to the success of the participants. Interestingly, work by De Pater et al. (2010) supported previous research that suggested that women are given fewer challenging work assignments than men – so women need to make sure they put themselves forward for any projects or assignments that they see.

If you're in your first role, then you don't need to be particularly fussy in your choices of either your next role or a secondment. What we'd recommend in the first instance is moving around at the same level to gain maximum experience, so if you work in an academic department, try and move to a role in central administration or a student services function. As Jayne Dowden, Director of Human Resources at Cardiff University, says '[secondments are] the way that you actually build individual capability, but also institutional capacity'. This does, of course, need to be balanced with learning a role and staying in it long enough to contribute to that area of work. Amanda Wilcox, Senior

Advisor in the Pro-Vice-Chancellors' Office at the University of Hull, has this to say:

> There are times in your career where achieving a broad range of experiences rather than racing up the career ladder is important. Employers understand that this gives you a deeper knowledge of your institution and of the sector. It is however important to be able to demonstrate the learning that you have acquired in each of your roles and to show how this learning will contribute to your next career move.

If you work in a specialist area such as finance, then this sort of moving around is perhaps more limited; but there will be opportunities to take on project work and this would expose you to different people and areas of the university as well as give you more institutional level thinking. Or you could leave your specialism behind and move into more general higher education administration. If you've gained a few years of experience and are feeling ready for a move up to the next grade, this will be easier if you have gained experience in different areas. Your first step up the career ladder need not be too strategic, but should at least try to offer the prospective employer some relevant skills and also plug a gap in knowledge. So, for example, if you've been working in quite specialised roles such as research administration or teaching support, then try to get a role that utilises all that knowledge and experience but perhaps is more strategic in approach so you also gain new skills. That said, we can't give hard and fast rules here. Ultimately, you will have to make a judgement based on your own views, values and circumstances, as well as on the institutional context.

Additionally, some international experience would be very useful. There are, of course, both similarities and differences between countries but moving between those such as the UK, USA, Canada, Australia and New Zealand would certainly be more straightforward than moving to countries with very different models of higher education – and language constraints, of course. Jon Baldwin, Deputy Vice Chancellor (Professional Services), Murdoch University, describes the five to six months he spent in the USA in his late twenties as 'extraordinarily valuable'. He goes on to say:

> I think just lifting somebody out of [their institution] and just letting them spend a month in UCL or Oxford or somewhere is incredibly valuable. So, that old generalist philosophy about administrators – about being able to move people around – I still hold to. If bright young staff experience different parts of your university, that's good; if you can give them a bit of experience in another institution,

that's better; and if you can give them some international experience, that's better still. I really wish we could [...] work something out that facilitated a more regular and rigorous exchange programme between, for example, a Murdoch and a Warwick or a Cardiff and a Melbourne...because it really benefits people greatly, I really believe that. It's much more complicated than it sounds; it's intuitively attractive, but the practicalities are quite difficult.

External opportunities

There are other ways to gain experience if your internal opportunities are a bit limited, or if you are seeking to expand your experience more broadly. One really good way to do this is to become a school governor or charity trustee. These types of governance roles expose you to conversations around strategic plans and finances, risk management, human resource strategy, key performance indicators – all the things that will stand you in good stead for more senior positions in higher education. There are many opportunities to become a school governor, and if you're not confident that you could go straight to board level and become a trustee, then this is a really good intermediate step and very worthwhile to boot – there is a dearth of school governors in some areas of the country, and they are crying out for interested and competent people to take on these roles.

If you've done this or feel confident enough, then you could apply for a trustee or non-executive director role of a charity. Many of these are advertised in the press, especially (for UK readers) in *The Guardian*, or through executive recruitment agencies or via the government's public appointments website. It's a little bit more intimidating, because more often than not you'll have to go through an interview process to be offered a position; but see this as good interview practice even if you don't succeed on your first go. Having interviews, even if you're unsuccessful (and you will be at some points), means that you get feedback on your performance and areas of developmental need; where interviews are concerned, practice does indeed make perfect. If you work in finance, the legal department or human resources, you'll be in even more demand with your specialist knowledge. If your career includes aspects of fundraising, then charities are often looking for volunteers to take this on, and you could learn a lot about fundraising and membership management from these organisations.

Professional bodies

An excellent way of finding new opportunities is to both join a professional body and to actively engage with its activities. In the UK, the main general body for all staff is the AUA. Higher education administration, of course, is a global business and countries with similar higher education environments to the UK have their own professional bodies such as Association for Tertiary Education Management in Australasia, the Canadian Association of University Business Officers and the American Association of University Administrators. These professional bodies all have similar objectives, in the main to professionalise university administration, and whilst this book cannot discuss all of these different professional bodies and does concentrate on the UK sector, much of what follows will apply elsewhere.

The AUA's objective 'is to advance and assist in the advancement of education by fostering sound methods of leadership, management and administration in further and higher education by education, training, and other means'. You can get involved with the AUA in a number of ways, which will probably differ dependent your career stage. For example, if you want to enter into the professional services or are just at the start of your career, then going to the annual conference to learn new things and to network will be invaluable. You could also attend your local branch's events, join a study tour (good for networking as well) or apply for a travel award. As you gain more experience in your career, you might want to give a session at the annual conference or write an article for the professional journal, *Perspectives: Policy and Practice in Higher Education*. You might also want to think about applying to become a Board Trustee or a member of Council: opportunities arise annually and any member can apply. Not only will you be learning new skills; you'll be offering something back to the body. There are plenty of other ways to get involved, so we would encourage you to join and make the most of your membership fee. As you gain more seniority, other professional bodies come into play such as the Academic Registrars Council (ARC) and/or the Association of Heads of University Administration (AHUA) which complement the work of the AUA.

There are other, more specialised professional bodies in the UK that complement membership of generic bodies like the AUA, such as the Association of Research Managers and Administrators (ARMA); AMOSSHE, The Student Services Organisation; the Chartered Management Institute (CMI); and the Institute of Leadership and Management (ILM). Staff working in, for example, finance or human resources, have their own professional bodies such as the Chartered Institute of Personnel and Development (CIPD) or Chartered Institute of Management Accountants (CIMA). In the USA, other more specialist professional bodies include NASPA – Student Affairs Administrators in Higher Education and the National Association of Student Financial Aid Administrators (NASFAA).

▶ Conclusion

In this chapter, we've explored some of the tangible activities that you can undertake to help progress your career. This chapter is a combination of our experience and what people we've spoken to for the case studies have reported, backed up by some evidence in the literature. Of course, we're not guaranteeing that everyone who reads this chapter and follows the advice will become the next Registrar of their university! However, what we hope it shows you is that there is a lot we as individuals can do to manage our career development and that there are good reasons why we should spend time and resources (including our own) doing this. One of the key findings from the case studies is that being able to reflect critically on your own behaviours and skills, coupled with an idea of what you want to do next, is vital to being able to develop a relevant professional development plan. The next chapter explores how you can get others to help you in doing this by making good use of 'networks'.

▶ Note

1 Triple accredited means business schools accredited by all three MBA associations: AACSB (aacsb.edu), EQUIS (efmd.org), AMBA (mbaworld.com).

▶ Useful contacts

Academic Registrars Council (www.arc.ac.uk)

Ambitious Futures (www.ambitiousfutures.co.uk)

American Association for University Administrators (www.aaua.org)

Association of Heads of University Administration (www.ahua.ac.uk)

Association of Managers of Student Services in Higher Education (www.amosshe.org.uk)

Association of Registrars of the Universities and colleges of Canada (www.arucc.com)

Association of Research Managers and Administrators (www.arma.ac.uk)

Association of Tertiary Education Management (www.atem.org.au)

Association of University Administrators (www.aua.ac.uk)

The Canadian Association of University Business Officers (www.caubo.ca)

Chartered Institute of Management Accountants (www.cimaglobal.com)

Chartered Institute of Personnel and Development (www.cipd.co.uk)

Chartered Management Institute (www.managers.org.uk)

The Guardian (www.guardian.co.uk)

Herzberg's Theory of Motivation (www.vitae.ac.uk/policy-practice/273431/Motivation-in-theory.html)

Institute of Leadership and Management (www.i-l-m.com)

Leadership Foundation for Higher Education (www.lfhe.ac.uk)

LH Martin Institute (http://www.lhmartininstitute.edu.au/)

Myers–Briggs (www.myersbriggs.org)

NASPA – Student Affairs Administrators in Higher Education (www.naspa.org)

National Association of Student Financial Aid Administrators (www.nasfaa.org)

Prince2 (www.prince-officialsite.com)

Public Appointments (www.publicappointments.cabinetoffice.gov.uk)

School Governors' One Stop Shop (www.sgoss.org.uk)

Taylor and Francis (publisher of *Perspectives: Policy and Practice in Higher Education*, www.tandfonline.com)

UCU pay scales (www.ucu.org.uk/index.cfm?articleid=2210)

▶ References

AUA (2013) Association of University Administrators, http://cpdframework.aua.ac.uk, accessed 23 March 2013.

Burke, J. M. and Attridge, M. (2011) 'Pathways to career and leadership success: Part 2 – striking gender similarities among $100k professionals', *Journal of Workplace Behavioural Health*, 26(3), 207–239.

Converse, P. D., Pathak, J., DePaul-Haddock, A. M., Gotlib, T. and Merbedone, M. (2012) 'Controlling your environment and yourself: Implications for career success', *Journal of Vocational Behavior*, 80(1), 148–159.

De Pater, I. E., Van Vianen, A. E. M. and Bechtoldt, M. N. (2010) 'Gender differences in job challenge: A matter of task allocation', *Gender, Work and Organization*, 17(4), 433–453.

Doherty, L. and Manfredi, S. (2009) 'Improving women's representation in senior positions in universities', *Employee Relations*, 32(2), 138–155.

Gander, M. (2010) 'Cracked but not broken: The continued gender pay gap in senior administrative positions', *Perspectives: policy and practice in higher education*, 14(4), 120–126.

The Myers & Briggs Foundation (2013) Type use for everyday life, www.myersbriggs.org, accessed 23 March 2013.

Raelin, J. A. (2002) ' "I Don't Have Time to Think!" versus the art of reflective practice', *Reflections*, 4(1), 66–79.

Singh, V., Terjesen, S. and Vinnicombe, S. (2008) 'Newly appointed directors in the boardroom: How do women and men differ?' *European Management Journal*, 26(1), 48–58.

4 Using Networks to Create Opportunities

▶ **Introduction**

Put simply, you could say that this chapter is the 'who you know' to Chapter 3's 'what you know'. Who you know – and who knows you – can play a significant role in managing your career. The chapter focusses on networks and networking in the context of higher education administration, whilst also acknowledging that some of the advice and observations may serve you equally well in other settings, both in a personal and a professional capacity. As with other parts of the book, you should be able to use this chapter to suit your own needs and ambitions, so if you're new to networking you may like to start by reflecting on the importance of networks and networking, and if you've got more experience you could go straight to the section on adding value to your networks.

This chapter will help you analyse the many ways that the word 'network' can be understood in our context of higher education administration and will get you thinking about why networks are important to you. As Liesl Elder wryly observes:

> It's easy to be the faceless, nameless administrator if you don't ever interact with academic or other colleagues. You can very happily come to work every day and do your job, and do a very good job of your job, and never know lots of people round the University. Ultimately that will hamper you because so much of what we do is personally driven, and I think if you're well known, people will understand that you're a good person (they may not like what your office is doing but they'll know that you're decent) so I think putting yourself out there is quite important in whatever format that is.

From there, the chapter puts that theory into practice to equip you to use your networks to enhance both your working life more generally and your career development more specifically. We consider how some of the senior higher education administrators we interviewed understand and use networks, including a case study from Canada.

Kirsten Gillingham reflects on the concern that the very word 'networking' can invoke:

> Everyone was going on about networking and how important networking was and I was thinking, 'I can't do networking, that's far too scary, I'm not that kind of person'...only to discover that's what I spend all my time doing, it's just I don't call it networking.

So we have some myth busting to do in this chapter as well, to show that:

- networking isn't always a separate 'thing' – and it doesn't have to involve wine receptions; and
- networking isn't a new phenomenon and it's not all about Facebook.

As Jon Baldwin puts it, networking is simply 'about good interpersonal skills, empathy, an ability to listen and an ability to follow up'.

In the UK, US and other developed economies, there seems to be an unwritten rule in contemporary workplaces that the louder you are, the better you must be (see Cain, 2012). People skills, teamwork, open plan offices – all are factors that on the one hand facilitate possibilities for you to meet and get to know other people. But on the other hand, that doesn't mean that everyone is comfortable with this way of working, and as part of this chapter we will explore how to bring out your networking skills even if you are the sort of person who recoils at the idea of small talk at the proverbial water cooler. We contend that everyone can find a balance and everyone is capable of learning new networking styles.

Understanding how you work best in a networking environment then leads to the next step of identifying your current networks. From a career management perspective, this kind of exercise can fulfil a number of purposes: to work out where the gaps are in your networks and to start thinking about how those gaps can be filled; to consolidate your current networks and understand where influence lies; and, in conjunction with broader thinking about your career development, to work out who in your network can help you get moving up – or along – the career ladder. We then review how you can add value to your networks by moving on from your networking comfort zone and consolidating and developing your networks.

Whilst career development planning is an important element of reviewing and enhancing the value of your networks, we'll also look at three broader (and potentially deeper) aspects related to managing your networking:

- planning what you want to achieve through a particular type or instance of networking;
- controlling your networking time: when and how should you be networking;
- managing your 'personal brand': what you tell other people, and how and what they can find out about you.

▶ The importance of networks in higher education administration

Networks are all about opportunities: creating opportunities and making the most of them. Networks are often seen as being for individual gain, both in career terms and skills/knowledge development: 'the more you can draw on a strong network of people and contacts, the more productive and successful you will be' (Halpern, 2005). But working in higher education adds another dimension of networking for mutual or collaborative benefit, which can be both within and between institutions. The purpose of what we do as higher education administrators is to support the development of knowledge in our students and our academics; networking, even on a small scale, can drive that endeavour forwards.

This is observed by Hugh Jones:

> I think that collaboration is an enormously valuable thing to do for anyone who is working in higher education. It really helps to develop those contacts, so any chance you get when you've got to go to a meeting about x, y and z to sit with someone and just chat is brilliant.

Collaboration creates social capital, that is 'everyday networks, including many of the social customs and bonds that define them and keep them together' (Halpern, 2005, p. 2). These networks matter because they add value both for individuals and wider groups.

So here, in summary, are six reasons why networks add value to you as a higher education administrator:

Get a better job

This is, perhaps, the most obvious objective for much networking activity. It's certainly an area where career guides and self-help books come into their own (see the References section for just a couple of examples). The concept is simple: the more people you know, the more career opportunities you will have. That's not just the quantity of people you know, but the quality of those contacts: their seniority in the organisation, their own contacts and connections, their decision-making authority and so on.

Improve your ability to do your current job

If you're not seeking to change job right now, networks can enhance your ability to do your current role. In his study of the challenges facing an Australian university, Duke argues that:

> Universities must encompass and incorporate many forms of partnership, networking and collaboration internally and externally. In this way they may turn the threat of an invasive and highly perturbed environment into an opportunity.　(Duke, 2001, pp. 104–105)

This applies not just to the way that higher education institutions are organised and run, but how the staff working within them operate. To cope with complexity and change, collegiality and networking styles have to be placed above managerialism. Table 4.1 is a summary of how Duke compares managerialism to a networking style.

Get to know other people, and let them get to know you

Have you ever looked someone up on LinkedIn, or phoned or emailed someone else to find out what they know about another person? The fact that you can do that is a major advantage of contemporary networking: if you've got a question or want to find something out, you've got a broader group of people to whom you can turn. As noted in the Introduction, though, it's not just about who you know. Houghton says: '[a]nother great advantage of networking is that it allows people to see you. Exposure is essential when it comes to getting on in the world'

Table 4.1　Duke on managerialism and networking in universities

Managerialism	Networking
Hierarchical	Participatory
Corporatist	Clusters
Vertical	Horizontal
Bureaucratic	Entrepreneurial
Control	Enable
Clients	Partners
Risk-averse	Innovative
Multiple managers	Leaders, administrators, facilitators
Bosses and workers	Colleagues

Source: Adapted from Duke (2001, p. 107).

(2005). This can not only save time – for example, in trying to initiate a contact – but can give you first-hand insight into specific roles in a university or help you find out who can give you that information.

Understand the wider higher education sector

Amanda Wilcox explains this point very clearly:

> It [networking] gives you a better and broader understanding of how the sector works and what the sector-wide issues are rather than just the institutional issues. It gives you an opportunity to get out of the institution, put your issues into context and realise that either everybody's having the same issues that you are – and there's a confidence or a comfort about that – or, you are the only one with that issue and it either means that you are inflating its significance or you should be learning from somebody else because they've already solved the problem. It's very difficult to see that when you don't look outside your own institution.

Develop and share good practice

This is where networking comes into its own as a public, as well as a private, good. In the next section, Mark Swindlehurst explains how his professional association enables all its members to share ideas, and in so doing, look at examples of good practice. Jon Baldwin talks about the unexpected advantages that this kind of networking can create: it makes 'people see the benefit of working together … not just the obvious areas to work together but in other sort of cross-boundary ways – academic/administrative, senior/junior … '.

In these types of networks, sometimes thought of as communities of practice, there is:

> a learning partnership among people who find it useful to learn from and with each other about a particular domain. They use each other's experience of practice as a learning resource. And they join forces in making sense of and addressing challenges they face individually or collectively.   (Wenger et al., 2011, p. 9)

For managers: Reinforce your team's skills

Managers should not be afraid to let people in their teams network actively. Kirsten Gillingham says:

> Now you might say for an organisation that that's not a benefit, but I think it is because if people feel empowered and they feel marketable, and they feel good at their job, actually they're more

likely to stay with you in some ways. You're more likely to lose people if they're feeling worthless and if they feel unvalued and demotivated and like they're not worth anything – you won't get good productivity out of them. But if they're feeling marketable and they've got good skills, they're out there and they can be seen, they're going to be doing a good job as well.

▶ Which types of network do senior higher education administrators use?

The quick answer to the question in this sub-heading is that there is no particular trend or pattern, and a lot depends on both the individual (e.g. their motivation and willingness to engage with different network types) and their role in the organisation (e.g. whether their role is very outward facing or more internally focussed). But even from this range of different responses, it's possible not only to pick out three of the key networking types used by senior higher education administrators, but also to gain an insight into how those networks add (or don't add) value to what they do. These network types are:

- informal networks;
- professional associations;
- virtual networks.

However, it's important to note that none of our interviewees use these networks in isolation; indeed, the network types can and do lend themselves to blended working. As an example, Case Study 4.1 shows the multiple ways in which the Canadian Association of University Business Officers (CAUBO) operates as a key networking tool, not simply as a professional association but through the multiple opportunities that membership offers or can be created by members.

Case study 4.1: Michael Di Grappa: Vice President, Administration and Finance, McGill University

For Michael Di Grappa, the benefits of his professional body are numerous:

> CAUBO provides many excellent networking opportunities for administrators. It offers forums for sharing experiences,

exchanging ideas and learning from others. It is a support group and a common voice on issues of common interest to all, or most, universities across Canada. It is a valuable resource for conducting research and for collecting information which can be shared with all members.

In 27 years of university administration, I cannot remember encountering a problem which someone else in a Canadian university has not encountered previously.

The opportunity to serve on the CAUBO Board [Michael Di Grappa is on the Board of Directors] is also a great experience as it brings me into closer contact with colleagues more frequently during the year and allows me to exchange with them and learn from the challenges they face. It also allows me to contribute to the continued health of the organisation.

I appreciate the opportunity to pick up the phone or send an email to someone I met through CAUBO and seek their opinion or feedback on a particular issue. I often check out the website for reports or resources. The annual conference is also a great opportunity to meet colleagues, learn from their experiences and discuss in formal and informal settings.

Many vendors and suppliers attend the annual conference and it is a great way to conduct business with them over a condensed period of time.

Informal networks

The importance of informal networks came up again and again in our interviews. Such networks may not be permanent or established groups, so serve a different function from professional associations. They can encompass a wide range of purposes, but quite often it's simply about having someone you can contact to ask for advice or for information. As such, this type of network can help you consolidate in the role you are currently in.

For example, Tania Rhodes-Taylor has built up an informal network of colleagues in the faculties at Queen Mary, University of London, for 'informal information exchange'. This can be a very effective way both to sound people out about an idea and for letting them know about a change before it is implemented.

As well as working with colleagues at your own institution, it can be very useful to know others in a similar position at other universities. As Hugh Jones says, '[i]t's very important to develop a bunch of people who work in different universities who will pick the phone up to you when you phone them and will just chat something through'.

Informal networks have a role to play in your career development too. Tessa Harrison recounts being interviewed for the position of Registrar at Southampton University:

> When I went for the interview at Southampton, the Vice Chancellor told me that I was the preferred candidate, but that it would be really helpful if they could get the view from other Russell Group Registrars. Well I know the majority of them and so I could ring up four of them and say 'Can you help me? Are you happy to talk to the Vice Chancellor at Southampton about me getting this job?'

Informal connections therefore act as facilitators and enablers and can help you do your current job better but also get from where you are now to the next step. And, as Dulworth says, 'peer-to-peer networking is the antidote to professional isolation' (2008, p. 101).

Professional associations

In Chapter 3, we looked at how professional associations can enhance your skill set. These associations also work in parallel with informal networks to achieve similar aims: to improve how you operate in your job and as opportunities to get yourself known with a view to career progression.

At the time of writing, Mark Swindlehurst was Chair of the Association of University Directors of Estates, which focusses on planning, management, operation and development of estates and facilities in UK universities. He draws a comparison between the way that professional associations and academic research operate:

> I believe you can benefit as an institution from sharing experiences... if you talk about collaboration and the benefit that collaboration brings from an academic research point of view, it's equally the same when you get into professional administration. If somebody has a good idea that the UK higher education sector can benefit from, we should be sharing that idea across the sector.

Liesl Elder, noting that 'networking is a big piece of what we [development/fundraising professionals] do', substantiates this by demonstrating the impact one professional association, the Council for Advancement and Support of Education [CASE], has had on her throughout her career:

> I've met a couple of future bosses through CASE so that's worked out well. Now that I'm more senior, I do a lot through CASE because I'm talent spotting. I enjoy being around advancement people, but it also serves me well to know a whole bunch of people because it helps me find other people and it helps me know who to talk to about things.

Chapter 3 also offers a range of links so you can find out more about the range of professional associations designed for higher education administrators in both generalist and specific roles.

Virtual networks

Email discussion groups/mailing lists
When people think about virtual or online networks, they generally think about newer technologies such as social media. These are important and are covered in the next sub-section. However, given that almost all higher education administrators spend significant amounts of time being office based, it is worth pausing to consider how the senior administrators we interviewed use email for networking. For example, Amanda Wilcox is a member of various email mailing lists covering areas such as complaints, discipline, admissions and recruitment. Wilcox discusses the benefits of mailing lists:

> It's a useful way of keeping in view what discussions are going on in the sector so in that sense these mailing lists add value because you can read them very quickly, you can filter them, you can plant them in your head and know what's happening externally. And you can do that and stay in the office!

Email groups can also allow you to keep in touch with others between face-to-face meetings and thereby enhance the value of a network; and they can act as an alternative to face-to-face networking, as Kirsten Gillingham explains:

> I'm a member of the Universities, Colleges and Academies Panel, a committee of my professional institute the Chartered Institute of Public Finance and Accountancy. They meet three or four times a year in London. I don't make all the meetings but I try and make one or two a year. There's an email list and that's somewhere where I'm in touch with a broader community.

Social media

Quite a few of our interviewees use one or more forms of social media-enabled networks, with the most frequently discussed being LinkedIn, Twitter and blogs. Acknowledging the burgeoning array of social media-enabled networks, the aim here is simply to give an illustration of how these three networks can be used in a higher education administration setting. If you're interested in finding out more about how these types of networks operate, there is a list of useful web-based learning resources at the end of this section. No social media-enabled network adds anything new to the basic principles of networking, but what they can do is enable you to network in a more innovative way, and that's what makes them valuable. For example, if your networks stretch across more than one country because of the work you do/have done, and/or your expertise ranges over a number of functional areas/interests, social media-enabled networks can bring your contacts and expertise together, helping you keep track of everything in one place and perhaps even offering the possibility of creative new partnerships or connections between those different areas.

LinkedIn bills itself as 'the world's largest professional network' (www.linkedin.com/about-us). For our interviewees, it:

- helps them broaden their contacts in a particular area, by connecting to people who know people they already know. Kirsten Gillingham uses LinkedIn as her main social media-enabled network: 'I've been fairly active in reaching out and making links with people and when people want to link with me, as long as they're relevant to my job, I'll accept them';
- helps them with recruitment, as they may already have come across a job candidate through LinkedIn. As Liesl Elder noted: 'if their CV crosses my desk, I'll remember that I know who this person is because I've seen them on LinkedIn'. For more junior members of staff, this can work in the other direction: if you are already connected to a potential employer on the network, it may help your application to stand out;
- allows them to 'find out what other people are up to' (Tania Rhodes-Taylor), thus enabling them to keep up to date with information about colleagues who they may not have opportunities to see or speak to in other settings.

A small number of our interviewees mentioned **Twitter**, which calls itself a 'real-time information network that connects you to the latest stories, ideas, opinions and news about what you find interesting' (https://twitter.com/about). Liesl Elder started using it when the conference she was chairing asked participants to tweet about the conference. Whilst she was initially sceptical about using it, she now finds it a useful tool for many of the same reasons as LinkedIn can help. Incidentally, this adaptation process, starting with denial and anger is apparently common – see a light-hearted take on this at www.mediabistro. com/alltwitter/getting-twitter_b9660. Elder makes an important observation about her use of Twitter: 'whatever I'm doing on social networking, it's public' and this is explored in the section on managing your networking later in the chapter.

Paul Greatrix's primary motivation for starting his *Registrarism* **blog** (http://registrarism.wordpress.com) was to communicate better with others working at the University of Nottingham, which is like many other universities in that it is a large and devolved institution with staff located at a number of sites (including China and Malaysia, as well as across Nottingham). A blog allows you to keep what is effectively an online diary and input and share stories as often as you want. Greatrix observes that 'as an internal communications device, it's largely failed', but that, unexpectedly, it has had other benefits. The blog 'serves as a terrific vehicle for telling the world what you think about stuff and creates interesting connections with people that I wouldn't ever otherwise have come across...'. That includes these authors, who connected with Greatrix after following his blog. Whilst Greatrix acknowledges the importance of his support network of other university Registrars, it is clear that the wider connections he makes through the blog offer a forum not just for him but for blog readers to discuss and analyse higher education administration, and in so doing extend their learning and enhance their sense of professional identity.

It's worth noting that **Facebook** doesn't feature at all as important for the administrators we interviewed. Its value is perceived to be primarily social and generally not used for professional purposes. Nonetheless, Facebook is mentioned here to acknowledge its status as the most heavily used network type, which in some circumstances can make it a useful mechanism to reach out to people. In 2013, over one billion people worldwide use Facebook, whereas LinkedIn has over 200 million users. Given that Facebook has a deliberately broader appeal than work-related LinkedIn, this is understandable, but the point is that you are much more likely to find someone on Facebook than LinkedIn. The question to ask yourself is whether you want to do anything about that, and whether Facebook is the right forum for any kind of professional networking.

Find out more

This isn't an exhaustive list and by the time this book is published, the networks *du jour* may well have changed. The choice of resources below is therefore based on what has proven to be popular and well used by higher education administrators in recent years.

Run by a UK-based educational developer whose current research is on the use of **social media** within higher education, you won't get much more context relevant that Sue Beckingham's *Social Media 4 Us* at http://socialmedia4us.wordpress.com. Subtitled *Getting started with social media*, the blog brings together articles, videos and Sue's own tips on interacting with LinkedIn, Facebook, Twitter, Google+ and other communication and collaboration tools.

See also Beckingham's presentation from the Association of University Administrators' 2012 Conference, *Social media for the terrified: the donut theory*, at www.slideshare.net/suebeckingham/aua12-social-media-for-the-terrified. (Why donuts? See the American site http://threeshipsmedia.com/blog/social-media-and-donuts – and for those of you who are fed up of too much technology, note that the donut analogy is explained using a good old fashioned flipchart).

One of the best **email mailing lists** for higher education professionals is run by Jiscmail, www.jiscmail.ac.uk. Although Jiscmail is UK-based, it is used in over 200 countries worldwide and popular in Germany, the USA, Canada and Australia. It has a very helpful 'how to' and 'what for' guide at www.jiscmail.ac.uk/about/whatisjiscmail.html.

Reliable sites for creating a **blog** include http://wordpress.com, www.blogger.com (now owned by Google) and https://www.tumblr.com. If you're interested in blogging but don't know where to start, try: www.bbc.co.uk/webwise/guides/how-to-get-a-blog, or google 'how to start a blog'.

▶ **What are your networks?**

Your networking comfort zone

Your networking comfort zone is a way of thinking about how you position yourself in relation to networking. Being in a networking comfort zone means you feel in control of your networks and how you go about networking. It's important to reflect on this in order to understand whether your current networking comfort zone is enabling you to get the most of the opportunities that networks can offer. If it's not, you need to think about steps you can take to do more with your networks. It's also about recognising that as well as moving out of your networking comfort zone, there will be merits to staying in it, too. Overall, you should be aiming for what Canadian networking company Shepa Learning (2013) calls 'productive discomfort', that is being neither too comfortable nor uncomfortable.

Undoubtedly the main concern that most people have when it comes to networking is the idea that they're no good at it or, as Kirsten Gillingham noted at the start of the chapter, that it's an overwhelmingly scary prospect. If this describes you, the questions you need to ask yourself are:

- Why do you think you are no good at this?
- What types of networking make you nervous? (And what do you think makes other people nervous? They may be trying to network with you!)
- What are you networking for?

There will be ways of networking that you already engage with, for example something as straightforward as discussing a work issue with colleagues (yes, that does count as networking), or as Tessa Harrison points out: 'I'm just naturally curious and I really like meeting people and finding things out really. I like to know more than just what's going on in the day job'. Networking is about much more than walking into a crowded room and having to find someone talk to.

However, remember that just because something is available doesn't mean you need to use it. As Tania Rhodes-Taylor puts it, 'I thought about doing a blog but I have enough difficulty trying to think up tweets!' It's important to remember that none of the senior higher education administrators we interviewed use hundreds of different ways of networking: the trick is to understand which types of networks are effective for you, and which you can work with best. It's absolutely legitimate to use several types of networks to achieve either the same or different aims.

That is not to say it's not possible to start using new networking styles, and in particular there are now a lot of social media-enabled networks that you may want to explore. The section later in this chapter points you to some good learning resources that could help you take a first step into a new network type. Alan Burrell reflects:

Personally I don't use social media, it's not useful for networking in my circles, but if I was looking for a career move now I would engage with it. Probably the only reason I haven't is I'm too near retirement to start worrying about it but I think it is probably becoming more vital.

Another point to remember is that you don't have to try and do every-thing: just as your contacts should be high quality rather than high in volume, similarly the quality of your networking is much more critical than the quantity of networking you do. Amanda Wilcox reflects on her external networking as a reviewer for the Quality Assurance Agency and as a member of the Academic Registrars' Council:

> If people are trying to nurture their career, I think having at least one external component to your bow is really important. It's really good if it could be something that's relevant and there are enough opportunities out there but I think if you're going to do it, you need to do it well. I always think if I can't do it well, I'm not going to do it at all. So I don't usually overflood myself with these things. I think some people do and then I'm not sure that they can do the job they're supposed to be doing plus all these external things.

Mapping your networks

Here are two mapping exercises you can do to identify who is in your networks, as well as what types of network you feel most comfort-able whilst using. These are worth doing whatever your career stage because you will always benefit from knowing which individuals and groups can support your work and improve your team's/organisation's work. As the Association of University Administrators' Continuing Pro-fessional Development framework notes: 'Information and knowledge are sometimes neglected as key resources. Anything that helps you and/or others to learn or improve is a vital resource' (Shine, undated).

First, understanding who you can count in your existing networks. Networking literature suggests you make lists of people you know already in the following categories:

Primarily social networks

- Friends, family, neighbours;
- People you know from face-to-face or virtual groups or organisa-tions you belong to, for example, sports, hobbies, volunteering.

Primarily professional networks

- Work colleagues and former work colleagues;
- People you've met at conferences, work-related groups you belong to; for example your regional branch of the Association of University Administrators, a LinkedIn group or an email mailing list (for more on this, see e.g. Dulworth, 2008 or Kay, 2010).

Remember that people you know can be part of both social and pro-fessional networks and that you may know them well or may never have met them in person before. They all count towards your current network map.

In addition to this, you could consider adding further detail to each of the people you've identified. Anne Hall, a UK-based higher education consultant at HE Interims Ltd, suggests keeping a list with their contact details, the date you last contacted them (or they you) and the purpose of the contact. She also suggests using 'hot', 'warm' and 'cool' contacts (colour coded on your list) to represent the strength of your relationship with the contact. So a 'hot' (red) contact would make a real effort on your behalf, for example helping you to brainstorm a list of people you could talk to about a particular role and then helping you get in touch with them. A 'warm' (amber) contact would be someone you know quite well but perhaps don't see that often and a 'cold' (blue) contact may give you information but not much time. All of these 'temperatures' are useful at some point or another.

The second exercise helps you understand how you network at the moment. List out the different ways that you could network in your role as a way of distinguishing the networking types that work for you. Start by using the three areas described in the previous section that are well-used by senior higher education administrators – informal networks, professional associations and virtual networks.

As an extra dimension to the second exercise, you could visualise how often you use each network type. List the instances of networking you've used under each type over the last year, so, for example, under informal networking you might include: lunch with A, phoned up B to ask about X project, emailed C with a question about Y...and so on. You could either do this on in a spreadsheet with types in a row and then each instance in a column underneath or you could cut and paste the words into a Wordle (www.wordle.net/create) or another visualisation tool. Either way will show you where your highest frequency networking takes place. You can then consolidate on your strengths and start to think about how to develop in other areas.

▶ Adding value to your networks

Moving on from your networking comfort zone

Sometimes you just have to feel the fear and do it anyway. On this, Hugh Jones says:

> I feel really uncomfortable when you've got the big conference and the fifteen minutes for coffee before you start off there. I hate that sort of chat. I'm not very good at it, I feel very shy...If I'm in front of stage talking to 100 people, I can do that no problem at all. I can

talk one-to-one, fantastic, no problem, and in small groups, but in a big room? I really don't like it. But you have to do it.

And Tania Rhodes-Taylor explains why you have to push your boundaries:

> There's nothing else you can do. You can stand in a corner and look scared – I tried that strategy for a couple of years, but then you just get all the other scared people. Sometimes that can be beneficial and sometimes it can't. I don't like it [walking up and saying hello], I have to admit I'm not one of these people who can just walk into a room and command it, it's just not my style, but I take a deep breath and I go and say hello to people.

To prepare yourself for the wine reception moment, set yourself what Shepa Learning (2013) calls 'networking stretch goals' which start to take you beyond your networking comfort zone. For example, at a meeting or event with a question and answer session, ask a question. The next time you do it in an environment where people don't know you, use your full name – and maybe even mention the department you work for.

You could then move on to tackle one or more of the three challenges for the higher education community developed by the University of Venus. These are also good if you want to reinvigorate your own networking. You may need to adapt the challenges depending on your role, but we believe that the premise of 'reach out, make contacts and go international' is achievable in some form or another for everyone. In summary, the challenges are:

- Go interdisciplinary – meet someone outside your department/unit;
- Go international – if your work doesn't put you in contact with students or universities outside of your country, try connecting through your international office or via an online networking group;
- Go outside your institution – to a neighbouring institution and to your local community.

See http://uvenus.org/about/challenge/ for more details and www.insidehighered.com/blogs/networking-aka-getting-outside-comfort-zone for an example of how this worked for one US based contributor.

In the section below on managing your networking, you may also like to use some of the ideas about your personal brand to help you develop beyond your comfort zone.

It's important to reward yourself for your efforts. In her fascinating book on how to get the best out of different personality types, Cain gives some valuable advice:

> Figure out what you are meant to contribute to the world and make sure you contribute it. If this requires public speaking or networking or other activities that make you uncomfortable, do them anyway. But accept that they're difficult, get the training you need to make them easier, and reward yourself when you're done…Here's a rule of thumb for networking events: one new honest-to-goodness relationship is worth ten fistfuls of business cards. Rush home afterwards and kick back on your sofa. Carve out restorative niches.   (2012, pp. 264–265)

Building up your networks

The senior administrators we interviewed offered a number of ideas that you could use to build up your networks and networking literature is also full of tips. Here are their – and our – top suggestions to help you build your networks, and an exercise you can do to assess the value that your networking is providing you with.

- Join relevant external groups: 'It is important that you network in those areas where your expertise lies, e.g. there's a cleaning group, a security group etc. This is how you find out about jobs, how you can get known, and it looks good on the CV' (Alan Burrell).
- Enrich your local networks:

  > I make sure I go to committee meetings and when there are more social events, I go to those. I join a sub-committee, I get involved in stuff and interact with email exchanges so I'm seen to be an active player. Through that, there are other little networks that develop through that whole community: I'm part of a sub-network of more local colleges, I go and have lunch or invite people into lunch just one-on-one to catch up with issues. (Kirsten Gillingham)

- Use your existing contacts: 'One of the ways I've done it is through my mentor, who has introduced me to various people which has helped broaden my network' (Tracy Carlton).
- Be specific if you are asking for advice:

  > At a recent training programme I saw a friend of mine who's the Registrar at another university. I went over to see him and I said, 'I've got a real problem with X issue and just don't know what to do about it.' We talked it through and he told me what he

was doing and how he was approaching it. So now I know I've got a specific thing I need to do following on from that.   (Tessa Harrison)

- Follow up and reciprocate: be prepared to offer someone a cup of tea or coffee or lunch and an hour of your time. 'As well as networking yourself, be receptive to people who say "can I borrow your time". Be generous and it will pay itself back' (Hugh Jones).
- Use business cards: 'I don't think university administrators are necessarily quite good at that, but get business cards and use them. Because it gives you a way to remember contacts and it actually gives you status as well, which is very important. And everyone's mum loves to see business cards!' (Hugh Jones).
- And last, but certainly not least, navigate your way around the dreaded wine reception: 'If people are already talking in groups, I won't shoulder in on that, but if someone's standing in a one or a two, I'll go and introduce myself and say hello. Normally to get rid of you, they'll introduce you to someone else!' (Tania Rhodes-Taylor).

In their study of value creation in communities and networks, Wenger et al. offer a series of key questions that allow you to reflect on the value of those networks, both to you as an individual and to the network as a greater whole. You could use these questions, which we've based on their five 'cycles of value', to review the effectiveness of a particular network type that you have become involved in.

- Cycle 1 – Immediate value: What happened and what was my experience of it? What was the quality and relevance of the activity/interaction? With whom did I make connections? Which connections are most influential on my own development?
- Cycle 2 – Potential value: What has all this activity produced? Have I acquired new skills, knowledge, methods or processes? Do I feel less isolated in my professional area? Have we (network) acquired a new voice through our collective learning?
- Cycle 3 – Applied value: What difference has it made to my practice/life/context? Where have I applied a skill I acquired? When did I leverage a network connection to help accomplish a task?
- Cycle 4 – Realised value: What difference has it made to my ability to achieve what matters to me or other stakeholders? Did I save time or achieve something new? What has my organisation been able to achieve because of my participation in the network?
- Cycle 5 – Reframing value: Has it changed my or other stakeholders' understanding and definition of what matters? Has the process

of social learning led to a reflection on what matters? Has a new framework or system evolved as a result of this new understanding? (Adapted from Wenger et al., 2011, pp. 22–23)

▶ Managing your networking

Managing your networking has three aspects to it: planning your objectives, controlling your time and managing your 'personal brand'.

Planning what you want to achieve through a particular type or instance of networking

The Association of University Administrators (AUA) sent its members a series of emails ahead of its 2013 Annual Conference, one of which was titled 'Five easy tips for networking at the AUA Conference'. Their very top tip? 'Networking – like anything else – is a whole lot easier if you do a bit of planning... Have an objective. Make a plan'. Kay agrees: 'think about what you would like to achieve... What information do you wish to convey? What information would you ideally like to receive? What do you want the other person to do as a result? Organize yourself beforehand, be positive and keep the message simple' (2010).

However, there is also something to be said for using networking opportunities in a more spontaneous way. Sometimes *not* planning a networking strategy for a particular event that can work out to your advantage, as Tania Rhodes-Taylor shows in this example:

> I went to an event recently and I sat next to someone and just introduced myself. It turned out that he was an academic lead on quite a significant development that's taking place in the east end of London that we [at her university] would very much like to meet with, so he's coming in to meet our senior executives.

Your knowledge of your own area and of your institution's priorities can turn a chance encounter into a serious work-related development.

Controlling your networking time

Against the inevitable context of busy work and personal environments with overlapping priorities, you need to decide how much time you spend on your networks. As Michael Di Grappa explains:

> Networks require attention. You have to make an effort to stay in touch, to contribute to discussion, online or in person, and to bring value for the other members. The biggest obstacle is time. It seems

like we are moving from crisis to crisis, with very little time for reflection and planning. That is where networks can be so helpful and beneficial.

Factors to take into consideration include:

- The nature of your current role: People working in, say, events management or fundraising may find they have more naturally occurring opportunities to build or develop networks than someone in a small, specialist team working only with internal stakeholders. The skills required for some roles may make networking easier, whereas in other roles you may need to invest more time understanding and learning about networks.
- The seniority of your role in the department/organisation: As you progress to more senior roles in higher education administration, you will have more control over how you use your time. We asked Paul Greatrix, a frequent blogger, whether someone in a more junior role could expect to be able to write blog posts during working hours. Greatrix said:

  > They've got to be really careful. I can manage my time much more easily, I can justify it. Frankly I think they've got to do it in their spare time because otherwise their manager might look at them askance and ask what they are doing. If they're doing something that is overtly related to their job, and is in the interests of promoting the department or the university, then they can absolutely justify it, but I think it's much harder. Having said that, I would still strongly encourage them to do it...

- When the networking happens: Is it during working hours (e.g. checking an email mailing list), over a lunch break (e.g. a lunchtime seminar) or during the evening (e.g. a dinner or reception) or even at a weekend (e.g. a conference)? The timing of a networking activity is important because you need to decide whether it is worth spending time – and possibly money – on it, inevitably in place of something else.

  Kirsten Gillingham is thoughtful and focussed in her approach:

  > I don't spend time on networking that isn't useful for work. If I'm going to an event or something there'll be content in it that's relevant that I actually want to go and listen to and pick up. Most activities aren't single purpose, so it's more a matter of planning in activities that are also networking so you're getting that kind of double benefit.

Managing your personal brand

Research shows that we are capable of creating a consistent first impression within 390 milliseconds (Bar et al., 2006). We all 'know' this, as we all make snap decisions about people when we first meet them using both conscious and unconscious clues. Your 'personal brand' will let people know what you offer above what your CV says: after all many people have degrees and skills training, but you need something that will differentiate you.

Jennifer Holloway, a personal branding expert, says that personal brand consists of values, drivers, reputation, behaviour, skills and image (2013). These can be split into two components – tangible and intangible. The tangible parts are easier to manage, so ask yourself what your image conveys about your brand, what skills you can offer beyond your qualifications and how your behaviour promotes you. Reflect on what you want your behaviour to say about you. Also, think about what you can offer if you're going for a new job or a secondment above your qualifications and skills. Are you known for, or do you want to be known for, getting things done or work with people collaboratively? What skills or qualities are important in your institution and how can you start to incorporate them into your brand?

However, the other components are intangible and need more work. What is your reputation, what do people say or think about you when you're not in the room? Are you consistent in all your behaviours? Do you always meet your promises? What are your drivers, what matters to you and motivates you? What are your values? So, if you want a promotion, think about how you can manage your brand to help you with this, to help people see beyond you in your current role, to seeing you as someone who can take on new levels of responsibility. However, don't forget that authenticity is key. You cannot manage your brand to be something you're not – people can see through this easily. There is no substitute for working hard, being trustworthy and having an excellent reputation but you can help the process by having the right voicemail messages, responding to emails promptly and professionally, ensuring your LinkedIn profile promotes you (authentically of course), your performance in meetings or when giving presentations. Every part of your work goes to make up your brand and people remember this – make sure that what people remember is what you want them to.

Managing your brand is especially relevant to the use of social media-enabled networks as you need to carefully consider what you tell other people and what they can find out about you. If you are using networks to get ahead in your career, then your future employer may be using the same networks to find out more about you.

Liesl Elder and Paul Greatrix have good advice to offer on your online network identity:

> My persona is always a public persona. I can't think of what my nickname would be other than Liesl Elder! So I feel that whatever I'm doing on social networking, it's public. If it's something personal, for example something about my cat, it would never be anything I would find embarrassing for work colleagues to find out. I think that's a good general rule.   (Liesl Elder)

> Always think about what happens when other people read it [what you have written online e.g. in a blog]. It's a good discipline and a good way of getting yourself visible but you do have to be more careful. If in doubt, ask a friend to read it first...I try and avoid overt politicisation regardless of what my own personal views are, and I always think – if this appeared in the Times Higher, would it embarrass my university? I do constantly reflect on that and I think that is actually really rather healthy because I'm always criticising myself, challenging myself on a daily basis and I think that's probably in my interests to do so.   (Paul Greatrix)

▶ Conclusion

It has been said about universities as a whole that they 'gain confidence when their self-image is confirmed by others – in the worldwide market, the local community, or groupings of similar universities' (Barnett, 1999, p. 101) and this analysis also works on an individual level. Our self-image can be confirmed by becoming involved with networks and then confirmed by others at a range of levels (local meetings, national conferences, online groups etc). This chapter has offered examples of how senior higher education administrators use networks, how you can understand your current networks and move towards developing them to help you become more effective, and why networks are important. Networks are not just for career progression but can enhance your ability to do any job with a deeper understanding, enjoyment and motivation. In the next chapter, we turn to another type of relationship that can have a massive impact on your work life in universities – the relationship between managers and those people and processes that they manage.

▶ References

Bar, M., Neat, M. and Linz, H. (2006) 'Very first impressions', *Emotion*, 6(2), 269–278.

Barnett, R. (1999) *Realizing the University in an Age of Supercomplexity*, Buckingham: SRHE & Open University Press.

Cain, S. (2012) *Quiet: The Power of Introverts in a World that can't Stop Talking*, London: Penguin.

Duke, C. (2001) 'Networks and managerialism: Field-testing competing paradigms', *Journal of Higher Education Policy and Management*, 23(1), 103–118.

Dulworth, M. (2008) *The Connect Effect: Building Strong Personal, Professional and Virtual Networks*, San Francisco: Berrett-Koehler Publishers Ltd.

Halpern, D. (2005) *Social Capital*, Cambridge: Polity.

Holloway, J. (2013) 'Managing your personal brand', webinar for Open University MBA alumni.

Houghton, A. (2005) *Finding Square Holes: Discover Who You Really Are and Find the Perfect Career*, Carmarthen: Crown House [accessed electronically].

Kay, F. (2010) *Successful Networking: How to Build New Networks for Career or Company Progression*, London: Kogan Page.

Shepa Learning (6 September 2013) Networking out of your comfort zone, http://shepalearning.com/networking-out-of-your-comfort-zone/, date accessed 25 November 2013.

Shine, J. (undated) Using resources – *AUA CPD Framework*, http://cpdframe work.aua.ac.uk/content/using-resources, date accessed 26 August 2013.

Wenger, E., Trayner, B. and de Laat, M. (2011) *Promoting and Assessing Value Creation in Communities and Networks: A Conceptual Framework*, Ruud de Moor Centrum, The Netherlands.

5 The Good Manager

Yes, the world is already achingly full of books on leadership and management. If you've read Chapter 3, you'll know that, if you haven't already done so, you're probably going to need to find some time to explore those shelves at some point. So no, we're not about to cover that ground here. Rather, the purpose of this chapter is to consider the place of 'the good manager' as you attempt to further your career in higher education administration. On one level, the value of this is obvious: for all that universities tend to be much less hierarchical than many other organisations of a similar size and scale, it's still unlikely that you will be able to progress beyond a certain point without taking on some management responsibilities.

It should go without saying, then, that being 'good' at it is going to matter – and for two key reasons: firstly, because how you approach the business of management will affect your own performance and therefore the story you are able to tell about your achievements and successes; and secondly, because the quality of the relationships you have with your own managers can make a big difference to your career progression. So far, so obvious perhaps. However, as we discussed in Chapter 2, there are some peculiarities of working in the higher education sector – some immediately obvious, other less so – that actually have profound effects on the way in which universities function in practice, and one of these is a distinctive approach to management, both conceptually and practically. The purpose of this chapter, then, is to explore what 'management' means in the higher education context, how it plays out in practice and the implications this has for our understanding of what constitutes a 'good manager' from an administrative perspective.

▶ The 'problem' of management in higher education

Consider this: according to the UK Higher Education Statistics Agency's data, in 2011–2012 students of 'Business and Administrative Studies' accounted for 18% of full-time first-year students in British universities. In the same year, a whopping 30% of all international students studying in the UK were undertaking business-related programmes. And the management schools delivering these programmes are, of course, staffed with academics researching the whole business of management, analysing organisational successes and failures and developing models from which others can learn. And yet few things get lips a-curling within a British university like the word 'management'. Indeed, 'management' and the 'managers' who practice it are regularly dismissed as insidious interlopers, hell-bent on destroying all that is good and noble about universities and their work. 'Management', in short, can be a very dirty word within universities.

One simple explanation for this would be that management involves control. As we noted back in Chapter 2, the notion that universities should require management at all is regarded by some as undermining to the very pillars of autonomy and academic freedom upon which the modern 'idea' of the university is built. A body of academic literature has emerged around the perceived threat to the integrity of universities posed by the rise of so-called 'new managerialism' – that is, the adoption of private sector management practices – in the past 30 or so years (e.g. Deem, 1998; Watson, 2000). This is not the place for a debate on the rights or wrongs of the managerial turn in universities – engage in that at your leisure, ideally at least sometimes in 'mixed' company in order that you understand how different categories of staff perceive and problematise 'management'.

For our purposes right now, Watson's observation that 'in a university nearly everybody manages something and in turn is managed by others' (2012, p. 42) is what matters. Given the vast array of activities that universities – willingly or not – are now performing, this is hardly surprising. And we already noted in Chapter 2 that the growth of the 'profession' on which this book focusses can, in large part, be put down to the increasing complexity of managing the university and gradual acceptance of the impossibility of distributing all of this workload around the academic staff whilst also expecting them to be actively teaching and researching. Nevertheless, Temple (2008) argues that we should be cautious about assuming that we can therefore simply import conventional ideas of what constitutes good and effective management into the university context, not because it is unwanted but rather because it is inappropriate.

We noted in Chapter 2 that a key feature of universities was the 'fuzziness' of their goals and this, Temple (2008) proposes, distinguishes them from the 'purposive' organisations on which much management theory is focussed: in the absence of an overriding, clearly measurable purpose such as generating profit, the task of management is not to push towards a common goal but rather to keep the institution together. In other words, universities are 'integrative organisations' and this in turn requires a different kind of approach that focusses on:

- making internal networks work well so that people at all levels know what is going on;
- 'Small–p' politics: 'The test of many decisions will be whether or not they work in political terms – whether they are broadly acceptable to key internal and, perhaps, external constituencies' (2008, p. 102);
- being impartial, because the absence of a clear purpose means that all claims for priority – for example, in access to resources – are likely to be justifiable in some way;
- devolution of decision-making, particularly in relation to budgeting – because it releases central decision-makers from at least some of the complexity of prioritisation.

One corollary of this, Watson notes, is that 'it remains true that almost everywhere the sphere of *self*-management in universities is wider than in comparable large and complex organisations' (2012, p. 42; authors' emphasis). A recent study for the UK's Leadership Foundation for Higher Education on the theme of academic *leadership* agrees, noting that academic staff typically work towards 'self-leadership' and look to their managers for the creation of 'an enabling environment in which they can pursue their academic work with fewer distractions and a greater connection to knowing and learning' (Bolden et al., 2012, p. 18) but that the greater emphasis on

> a corporate agenda in which universities are competing for funding and resources in a global marketplace and are responding through the adoption of more 'business-like' approaches to leadership, management and performance [. . . is] diminishing opportunities for academics to self-determine their own sense of *direction* and in so doing undermining their *commitment* to the institution and the profession.   (ibid, pp. 15–16)

This presents particular challenges for those in universities whose responsibility is explicitly to manage or contribute to the effective management of key university services, processes and resources. If it is true, as Bolden and colleagues claim, that '[t]he growth in professional services to support and complement the work of academics has, in many cases, not been associated with a corresponding increase in opportunities for staff in different groups to engage with one another', their proposed solution – that new processes and practices should be 'structured around academically meaningful activities' (ibid., p. 18) may be difficult in practice because not everything that needs to be managed is easily made so. As Tania Rhodes-Taylor of Queen Mary, University of London, observes:

> You don't want the great minds, who are looking into genome research and world health and relationships between Islam and the West, spending hours poring over their balance sheet wondering where the photocopying costs have gone. But somebody's got to worry about where the photocopying costs have gone!

▶ Management relationships and administrative staff

On one level, this academic resistance to being 'managed' may be of limited direct relevance to some categories of administrative staff. Particularly for those employed in what we might lazily describe as 'central' services, more traditional 'chain-of-command' style line management structures can and do operate. After all, hierarchies in universities may well be relatively flat compared with other large organisations, but they are less flat for administrative staff, whose roles cover many more levels of responsibility – grades, in shorthand – than is true of their academic colleagues. But it's not that simple, because we cannot just imagine management culture in universities as being easily separated into separate academic and administrative tribes that meet only in the office of the Vice Chancellor. Academic staff appear as managers of administrative staff at all levels, be that formally as line managers or via a range of other means that, whilst perhaps not unique to universities, certainly are sufficiently prevalent in them that we need to be aware of their implications for career development. Let's give some attention to these now.

The academic as line manager

There are three main circumstances under which you may find yourself being managed by an academic, as opposed to a more senior administrator, which, in reverse order of likelihood (no offence intended) are:

- Because you either *are* the most senior administrator in the place, that is, the Chief Operating Officer, Registrar or equivalent, in which case you probably report to the Vice Chancellor, or you are the Head of a service in an institution that does not have a unitary head of the administration and report either to the Vice Chancellor or a thematic Pro-Vice-Chancellor responsible for your area;

- Because you are employed to provide support to a specific academic project, typically but not necessarily a research project, and report directly to the academic leading it;
- Most commonly though it will simply be because you work in an academic unit (department, school, faculty, college) that is led by a member of academic staff who line manages you.

Allow us to park the first of these and concentrate on the second two, which are most relevant to those at junior and intermediate levels within the higher education career hierarchy. Academic-administrator line management relationships can be very positive and productive day to day. One of the major advantages of being in such a position is that it probably means you are working in one of what Tessa Harrison describes as the 'engines of the university' and as such are close to the academic action. Your opportunities to understand what universities are all about should be many and manifold. However, in terms of managing your career, there are some potential challenges of which you should be aware.

For instance, your manager may have only a limited understanding of what it is that you actually do all day (Matthews et al., 2006); indeed, they may regard at least some of what you do as externally imposed, pointless bureaucracy and want to have as little to do with it as possible! Conversely, even if they do understand and value your work, they may find it difficult to conceive that someone who is not an academic could possibly have the intellectual capacity really to comprehend what is required: academics can be terrible micro-managers. More likely, perhaps, they may have little awareness either of what they *could* be asking you to do or of what careers for administrative staff can look like. If you are lucky, they will be aware of their lack of knowledge; but don't rely on that. It's perhaps worth pausing here to acknowledge that the typical career pathway of an academic is such that they may be relatively senior in terms of pay scales before they actually become 'managers' themselves. Moreover, in some cases – and this is still relatively common in pre-1992 British universities, a 'Buggin's turn' (i.e. rotational) approach to Head of Department-type roles may operate and so they may have taken on a management role out of a sense of duty or just because 'there is no way I can cope with Dr/Prof X becoming Head' (Kennie, 2009, p. 9). Combine this with the academic preference for self-management and you may find that you are essentially on your own when it comes to your personal career development.

A note of caution: if you are brilliant, as we're sure you are, your academic line manager may not want you to leave. Ever. Being loved is all well and good, but unlike with academic staff, 'personal' promotions for support staff are unusual and there is a limit to the additional responsibilities that you can be given to facilitate a re-grading application without the real business needs of the department being compromised – remember those photocopying costs that need to be counted! As such, most of us will need at least to move around the institution, if not the sector, in order to achieve career progression.

But all is not lost: a key theme of this book is that you can (and should) take responsibility for your own career. Having an academic line manager is just something you need to work with; it's a normal feature of university life and is not something to be feared. This may be a point in your career where mentorship (see Chapter 6) may be particularly useful and also where accessing internal or external networks (see Chapter 4) can be a real boost. Thinking about opportunities to build links to other parts of the support services, for example, through short secondments or work-shadowing (see Chapter 3), could also help you understand the bigger picture. And you can always try to 'teach' your manager about your profession (we know a book they might read...!).

Requesting a 'dotted line' to an appropriate more senior member of administrative staff in 'the centre' may be an option (see next section), although be careful not to offend your academic in the asking (better perhaps to plant the seed and let them think the idea was theirs?!). And there is no substitute for being really good at what you do. Our interviewee Sarah Randall-Paley, whose higher education career has been at the centre and in a specialist area (Finance) is rightly concerned that 'it is harder for those in departments. Their roles are more generic. No one is looking out for their career progression and they have to move about more, rather than having an obvious career path'. On the other hand, a happy academic line manager, who understands and accepts that you will need to move *on* at some point to move *up*, can be your best champion within your institution.

'Dotted line' managers

One means by which universities commonly attempt to deal with the need to ensure the appropriate mix of academic and professional leadership for administrative roles is through 'dotted line' management relationships. The dots can run either way: you may be line managed formally by an academic but report to a more senior administrator for support and guidance, or your formal reporting may be to a member of administrative staff with your day-to-day workload driven primarily by an academic or academics (see Case Study 5.1 for examples of both models). Such relationships are usually more common at more senior levels: the higher up you go, the more likely that you will be responsible for delivering a significant element of the university's strategy that requires regular interaction with the responsible academic leader(s).

But they are not uncommon at less senior levels too, particularly for staff working in academic units or on projects.

Dotted line relationships work best when the formal and the dotted line manager(s) have a shared understanding of what is expected of you and the purpose of the dual reporting is to ensure that there is proper support for you to fulfil these expectations. Things may be more difficult where the dotted line has been put in place to stop you from 'going native' (i.e. becoming too influenced by your academic unit's agenda – an odd concern that suggests insufficient thought has been given to what universities are for and where support staff fit in, but don't underestimate the significance of 'centre-periphery tensions' in universities) – or because the academic manager doesn't want (or has proven themselves unable) to do 'the management' bit. Equally, if your dotted line is to a relatively random person at the centre, which is very possible if you are in a *generalist* role within an academic unit, it may be a very perfunctory relationship. And if there is more than one dotted line, you may find yourself pulled in many and competing directions (see the section 'Matrix management').

Case study 5.1: Heather Moyes, Business Manager, Vice Chancellor's Office, Cardiff University

When she took up her first post as Faculty Administrator at Lancaster University, Heather Moyes was based in the Academic Registrar's Office but had particular responsibility for the then Faculty of Social Sciences:

> My line manager was the Academic Registrar, but most of what I did was determined by the agenda of the Faculty, so I worked very closely with the Dean and the Associate Deans and mainly just kept my line manager informed as to what I was doing. A lot of what I did was committee servicing and so the workload set itself to some extent, although my line manager was really helpful in teaching me how to be an effective committee secretary. Then the University restructured into three much larger Faculties and part of this involved pushing more 'management' support out into the Faculties themselves. I took on the role of Faculty Manager for the new Arts and Social Sciences Faculty and my remit changed to become much more about providing strategic and operational support to the Dean and senior management team, as well as overseeing the Faculty Office.

At the same time, her line management was pushed out to the Dean, with a dotted line to a different senior member of administrative staff, this time within the Student Registry:

> During the transition year, the Acting Dean really wasn't making best use of me and was doing an awful lot that I could have been helping with. The University Secretary sat down with us and talked to him about the sorts of things that professional support could provide to him. It was like a revelation to him: he'd had no idea! It made a big difference both to him and to me; and I was able to take on new responsibilities, develop my own knowledge and skills and really get my teeth into supporting the Faculty's development.

In terms of the dotted-line relationship, this was perhaps less effective than it could have been:

> I'm not sure that the right person was given that responsibility because our areas of work didn't really overlap. At that point in my career, I really needed someone who could guide me in areas of work that were fairly specific. What was really useful was something that the University's Management Development Adviser encouraged the three Faculty Managers to do, which was to set up an action-learning set that she facilitated. We used it to share 'thorny issues' and provide mutual support. Our jobs were somewhat unique within the institution – providing a bridge between departments and 'the centre' – and we sometimes felt under attack from all sides! Having that supportive framework in which to offload and also to learn from each other and join-up issues made a massive difference in terms of our individual and collective effectiveness.

How much control and influence you have over the effectiveness of a dotted line management relationship and its impact on your career development will be partly a function of your seniority: the more senior you are, the less reliant you are likely to be on that relationship alone for development. But whatever your position, taking responsibility yourself will make a difference. The strategies we discuss elsewhere in the book apply – mentorship and networks can save your professional life! This is a time when coaching, covered in Chapter 6, can also be helpful.

And there is plenty of literature out there on the business of 'managing upwards'. Some key questions you might want to get answers to will include:

- Who sets your objectives?
- Who is going to do your appraisal? Will the other manager feed in to that somehow?
- From whose budget is any training or development you might require or wish to access coming?
- Who'd win in a fight? By which we mean, of course: who has greater call upon your time?

Centrally managed but locally embedded roles

An alternative to the dotted line relationship that is growing in popularity within British universities is to 'embed' centrally managed staff 'out there' in the academic units. This is more common for specialist staff in what we might call the 'established new professions' such as human resources, finance or IT, but it does also occur in areas like quality assurance/enhancement and research administration. It is probably more likely that the academic unit concerned will be a college or faculty than anything smaller, although this is not a hard-and-fast rule. The rationale for such an approach is that it improves communication and mutual awareness between centrally located, cross-institutional services and the academic units they are there to facilitate, allowing appropriate standards to be maintained whilst ensuring that these chime with what those actually delivering the academic agenda need.

The commonly expressed fear with such staff is that they will 'go native'; certainly, being an effective link between your professional area of expertise and the users of the service you provide requires a mixture of confidence and resilience to deal with mistrust from all sides. In terms of career development, however, as long as the practical issues we noted earlier with regard to objective-setting, appraisal and development needs are addressed, the strength of this approach is that what Sarah Randall-Paley calls your 'professional life' – and the field of practice from which you draw your expertise – is being explicitly acknowledged. Use that: make sure that you do work between the two.

Matrix management

This being higher education, don't think that the opportunities for complexity have been exhausted yet! Matrix management describes a situation in which the traditional chain-of-command hierarchy is replaced by a structure in which control – over people, processes and resources – is distributed horizontally as well as vertically. The two axes of influence, which we might call the 'organisational axis' and the 'thematic axis', exist in tension and, if that tension is properly calibrated, allow complex organisations to benefit from productive, creative, happy staff.

Cynics might dismiss 'matrix management' as just a way of putting a positive spin on the complex web of relationships that arise out of the cultural resistance to management within universities that we discussed at the beginning of this chapter. Certainly, circumstances in which academic members of staff discuss their research objectives with one colleague, have their teaching load allocated by another, report their leave to an administrator and day-to-day are not really answerable to anyone may sound familiar to many who already work in universities. Whether this is a fair representation of the reality is another matter: if the letters pages of *Times Higher Education* are anything to go by, universities across the land are clamping down on such practices and replacing them with draconian, quasi-militaristic command-and-control hierarchies. And there is another debate to be had as to whether matrix management works or not, but let's avoid getting into that here and keep focussed on you and your career development.

One of the advantages of a matrix model is that you come into contact with a wide range of people who have an interest in what you do and so could potentially be sources of support, guidance and advocacy for you. Many of these will be academic staff, so their awareness of your career trajectory may be limited; nevertheless, there are multiple opportunities to impress and be useful. The challenge, of course, will be that you are pulled in multiple directions by people who all want their piece of you, that it is not clear who you report to or who should be responsible for your training and development and that your workload gets out of control. There is an argument that matrix management works best for project-based work; others have suggested that the risk of degeneration into a morass of committees and complex rules is high (Bartlett and Ghoshal, 1990; Larson and Gobeli, 1987). If your role is about supporting these committees and rules, you may find yourself under pressure from all sides.

The following story by one interviewee (whom we are anonymising for obvious reasons) told of reporting in multiple directions is not uncommon:

> At times, I've been incredibly frustrated and wanting to scream. Other times, it seems to work quite neatly, where you end up having two advocates rather than one. But there are certainly occasions – and they are more than occasional – where those two people in this particular context here, the Registrar and the Pro-Vice-Chancellor, have very, very different expectations of what we are supposed

to be delivering or are due to deliver, and attempting to navigate this [is] challenging. I think you've got to [...] have a high degree of emotional intelligence, sensitivity, understanding of where it is appropriate to dig your heels in, which battles are worth fighting, seeing the long view. Not being upset by short-term campaign failures, if you like, with the long-term in view and then also, I think, being pretty magnanimous. You know, I can think of an incident just in the last couple of weeks where coming out of the Pro-Vice-Chancellor's mouth now is something which he refused to accept from me many months ago, but now it's his idea!

What to do? It's the same advice again: take responsibility for yourself. Seek out the people who can support you, take advantage of the matrix structure to be free to look for links that make sense for you. As with any role, be aware of your total workload and make sure that others are too. Unless this is a very radical matrix, you will still have a line manager and part of their responsibility will be to support you; but you may need to push on that. So push!

▷ Getting the most out of any management relationship

If there was any theme to the preceding section, it was: take responsibility. There is nothing special about universities in that regard: management relationships in any organisation have to be two-way streets to work and so the individual being managed has to be proactive. This is not to deny that bad line-managers and dysfunctional line-management relationships exist; on the contrary, almost everyone we interviewed for this book had had a mixed experience, be that because of a lack of support from their manager (a sense that their manager felt threatened by them, even) or because the management relationships themselves were poorly constructed. However, all also spoke of inspirational bosses, whose role in their career development was transformative. Jon Baldwin, for example, describes a passing conversation with a boss early in his career in higher education administration as a 'one of those moments of magical management' that gave him the confidence to progress.

For Hugh Jones, it was about learning good habits:

'X' [his first manager in higher education] was very, very clever and she taught me, I think, the value of listening; and the value of writing well and clearly and just how many doors that opens to you. Because if you can express yourself well and if you can write grammatically and spell properly and consistently you've passed the first test with an awful lot of academic leaders and therefore you will be listened to. And the lesson that comes from that is that, [...] although in lots of respects universities are very hierarchical places, in other respects they are very egalitarian places. One of the things I've found is that, if you have something interesting to say you, will be listened to, no matter who you are.

[...] I mean a good manager is a wonderful thing to have, an absolutely wonderful thing to have. It is actually remarkably empowering being told what you don't need to worry about. The really important thing I learned from 'Y' [a later manager] is the value of good enough and not doing perfectionism. Stop and do something else instead, if it has ticked the box. She also had good habits.

For Tessa Harrison – speaking of a dotted line, academic manager, please note! – it was about being pushed: ' "Z" was a huge supporter and advocate, and stretched me in ways that nobody has ever stretched me before intellectually and professionally'. For Andrew West, it was about being given opportunities to develop:

One of the tipping points, I think, in my career was a study visit I made to ten different universities in the United States, which was only over a period of a few weeks but has been significant in changing my practice and, I think, the department here. And you need support with something like that. [... Y]ou need a manager to say you can go; you need them maybe to give you a bit of money to help you.

And, of course, you can learn from 'bad managers' too. As another interviewee, again anonymised, explained of a boss earlier in her career:

[S]ome of the stuff she did with me early on, probably the first couple of years in post, [...] I found incredibly challenging and incredibly difficult. I mean she re-wrote everything I wrote, she picked me up on everything. Looking back, she probably more than anybody has made me the calibre of administrator I am today. I write well, you know, so I have to thank her for that, although at the time it was the most demoralising, confidence-busting experience. But I do look back on it and think actually, [...] she taught me a lot, she taught me a hell of a lot. She taught me to write, which I think in our context is really, really important [...]. I hadn't done a PhD or Master's, pretty rubbishy first degree, so she taught me how to write, which was important. I just wish she'd done it in a different way.

... [It's influenced me] hugely, really hugely. So now, for example, when other people are writing things for me, when I'm giving feedback, I always reflect back [...]. I lost my voice for a long time, because of the way [she] worked with me and I'm just beginning to find it, which is quite interesting. I'm very conscious of that, and I do say that to people, 'You know, I'm giving you this feedback, but I really don't want you to feel that I trying to squash your voice. If you don't agree with the change I'm making, that's absolutely fine. You've got to have your own style'.

▶ Being a good manager

So, one of the big things you can learn from your managers is the practices and habits that make them effective (or not) themselves. Some are obviously generic, but others are more relevant to the higher education context. We noted earlier the impact of the particular culture around management that commonly operates in universities. There is no doubt that 'the lack of power of managers (individually or in teams) to act upon their instincts without considering (some would say calculating) how to carry along with them the other individuals and groups with whom the share direct responsibility for the quality and the success of the enterprise' (Watson, 2000, p. 5) has implications for administrators as well as academic managers.

Jayne Dowden, Director of Human Resources, Cardiff University, puts it like this:

> Universities are quite interesting places to work because you're working in a less structured environment than in other organisations, particularly in relation to academic schools. In other organisations, you have managerial structures, which are acknowledged and where you have position power and people know who their line manager is [...]. They might actually have something to say about what you do! In universities, power is so much more negotiated. It's much more about – OK, you have position power, but that power actually only works if you have personal influence and credibility, and if you actually find the levers and make them work.

> So, from an HR perspective, it means that it's actually much more difficult to get anything implemented. You don't say, 'Do this' and

people do it, you say 'Do this' and people say 'Why?' and 'Couldn't we do it some other way? Wouldn't it be a better idea if we did it…?'. There's much more discussion and one has to adapt practice to actually accommodate that and actually involve people much more at early stages so that you actually do have a chance of rolling something out within living memory.

According to Peter McCaffery, a former vice chancellor and author of *The Higher Education Manager's Handbook: Effective Leadership and Management in Universities and Colleges*:

[T]here are more than a dozen important sources of power within organisations, ranging from the formal (such as control over resources and information, etc.) to the informal (such as interpersonal networks), and from the concrete (control over technology) to the abstract (the management of meaning and symbolism). In broad terms these can be categorised under four main types of power base: authority, expertise, resource control and interpersonal skill […]. Or, put the other way, from an individual perspective power comes from:

- Your formal position: your role;
- Your personal authority: the personal characteristics you have (articulacy, empathy, humour, intelligence, dynamism, physical appearance, etc.) that others find attractive or influential or persuasive;
- Your expertise: both real and imagined (by others);
- Your access to information;
- Your ability to recognise and seize an opportunity: to be 'in the right place at the right time'.

(2004, pp. 257–260)

Recognising these different levers and knowing what is appropriate when is particularly important in the higher education context, because, as Jayne Dowden noted, the chain of command is weak. Add to this the fact that universities are typically very large organisations that are held together as much by shared processes as by anything else. So, whilst you may manage a team of people, you may also be responsible for managing processes or resources which are used by people over whom you have no formal authority. Let's consider the challenges of these in turn.

Managing people well

Much of what makes a good people manager in a higher education con-text is generic: you need to listen, guide and advise, delegate well, set clear and reasonable objectives, trust people to perform and address any issues swiftly and fairly. And please don't do the same job as your team: your role is to coordinate resources, set and maintain standards, understand and communicate the context; that's why you are paid more. We won't bang on about that any further here (there are many, many books available on the subject); but we would strongly encourage you, depending on your career stage, to reflect upon and take seriously your approach to managing people and its effectiveness. If your team works well, it reflects well on you. As Harry Truman (possibly) once said, '[i]t's amazing how much you can get done, when you don't care who gets the credit'.

As for being a good manager in a university, it's worth highlighting four points. Firstly, it remains commonplace – in the UK at least – that people are thrust into management roles in universities without any training. This applies both to academic and administrative staff. How much you can really learn in the abstract and in advance about manag-ing people is debatable, but once in a role, many people find themselves crying out for support. It's usually there, if you look. Certainly, in the UK context, there has been significant investment in management train-ing in the past decade, both at local level and through organisations like the Leadership Foundation for Higher Education. The LH Martin Institute performs a similar role for those working in HE in Australia and New Zealand. Mentorship, as well as formal training, may also be critical and coaching can be a brilliant way of working through thorny issues around particular issues in your team (see Chapter 6).

Secondly, universities are typically large organisations and so there are many, many opportunities to be creative about getting the most out of your team. We talked in Chapter 3 about ways you can develop yourself: they are equally relevant to you in supporting your own staff to develop. To be sure, you may be nervous about letting people go off on secondment: in the short-term, you lose them as a resource; longer-term you might lose them completely. But, as Sarah Randall-Paley puts it, '[t]hey benefit everyone, because you get more resilience and skills within the team as a result. It's the same with mentorship: it has a two-way benefit'.

Thirdly, we noted earlier the risk that those with an academic line manager find themselves so 'treasured' that their careers stagnate because no one is encouraging them to think about their next move. For all that universities are big organisations, they are made up of many small parts and that 'loose-coupled' nature can encourage such a strong local loyalty amongst staff that they forget that there are opportunities in the wider university. We stressed earlier that you need to cast your net widely – whatever that might mean in your particular context; let your staff do the same. It's better to have two or three years of someone excellent who then moves on than to hold someone back because you fear life without them and see them lose their verve as a result. For this reason, Tania Rhodes-Taylor advocates including what she calls 'stretch objectives' as well as those more directly addressing current responsibilities.

Finally, universities are often criticised – both externally and by their own staff – for being really bad at performance management, by which what is usually meant is dealing with poor performance: 's/he wouldn't get away with that in the private sector' is a frequent refrain. Apart from the obvious observation that much 'performance management' happens in private – stocks in the main car park wouldn't go down too well in a tribunal now, would they?! – dealing with poor performance is challenging in *any* environment. That said, the focus on autonomy and self-leadership that underpins the prevailing culture around management at least as far as academics are concerned, combined with those 'fuzzy' goals we discussed in Chapter 2, may well account for an alleged reluctance to deal with under-performing staff in universities. However, this is an area that is being given much more attention across the sector – well or less well, we'll leave it to you to decide. The key thing to remember is that the only way to deal with poor performance is … to deal with poor performance! And that means you, yourself, as line manager, not human resources or someone else, you! Here endeth the lesson.

Managing processes

As for managing processes, services or resources, don't forget what they are for. Back in Chapter 2, we heard Jane Dowden highlight the importance of not simply doing great human resources, but rather delivering the human resources that the university needs in order to fulfil its mission. The same applies to student services; after all, without the students, where would we all be? In fact, whatever the focus on the service you provide, tying it back to the idea of the university and its purpose(s) it important. As Mark Swindlehurst says of his area of expertise:

> I think the role for Estates, for Facilities, is about creating communities at the institution that are really working together in the most effective way, so creating a community where you've got the best possible student satisfaction, staff satisfaction, visitor satisfaction. Because all that builds reputation. […] So my job

here is about asking 'how can I put in the facilities and services that create that community?' It's not just about bogs [toilets] and boilers.

Chapter 2 also discussed the tensions that turn on the question of what universities are for and what that means for who should run them. This applies as much with day-to-day processes as to missions and high-level strategies. For those managing services, achieving the appropriate balance between getting enough academic – and increasingly now student – input to defining desired outcomes and actually making things work along the way in the most efficient ways possible, is a constant challenge. This can be particularly tough in the context of processes that span both central and 'local' units: that loose-coupled nature we talked about earlier and the expectation of high degrees of autonomy for academic units can make for levels of resistance to the adoption of standard operating procedures across the institution that those coming from other sectors may find staggering. Being effective – and working out what effective means – in that context is not straightforward; understanding why it is so hard might help. As Hugh Jones observes,

> [t]here is something around the habits of mind that lead one to want to follow an academic career, [...] a curiosity and a desire to find out how things work, and the desire to [...] make it work better, and the confidence to do that, and indeed the ability quite often to do something which you are very good at. But nevertheless: can we please not reinvent operating systems for computers because that's been done already. And it's fine to make something up now, but are you, oh Professor Smith, going to be interesting in maintaining that every year when UCAS [UK's Universities and Colleges Admissions Service] do their updates? I don't think you are. And finding ways to let people express their curiosity and ideas, without actually saying 'but really don't do that'? It's part of the ongoing dialogue and one that can descend into a slightly patronising approach from both sides. And that's not helpful. I think it's important to understand the different drivers to get there...it's part of the question of 'how do you add value?'.

So proving your worth is important. But don't go too far: one of us, earlier in her career and somewhat terrorised by a self-imposed need to prove that her role wasn't simply an academic's salary gone astray, spent several weeks investigating the source of a ongoing smell of frying bacon that was causing a member of academic staff some irritation. Many abortive discussions with Estates, Residences and Catering later, she was eventually forced to report that there was nothing to be done … Only to discover that the academic in question, now having settled back in to campus life after a long summer of research leave, didn't notice it anymore! Keep an eye out for your own metaphorical bacon sandwiches.

▶ Conclusion

For all that higher education seems to struggle with the term, 'management' is a massive part of what goes on in universities and those in administrative roles will inevitably be involved in managing things, people and processes throughout their careers. They will also be managed themselves. In this chapter, we've sought to highlight some of the particular challenges and opportunities that arise from managing and being managed in the university context. We've emphasised the importance of being resilient and of taking responsibility for and learning from the quality of the management relationships that affect you. In the following chapter, we explore in some detail two tools that can be very important in helping you to cope effectively with these challenges: mentoring and coaching.

▶ Further reading

Borg, J. (2007) *Persuasion: The Art of Influencing People*, Harlow: Pearson Education.

Hall, A. (2003) *Managing People*, Maidenhead: Open University Press.

Lumby, J. (2012) *What Do We Know about Leadership in Higher Education? The Leadership Foundation for Higher Education's Research. Review paper*, London: Leadership Foundation for Higher Education.

Lundin, S. C., Paul, H. and Christiansen, J. (2011) *Fish! A Remarkable Way to Boost Morale and Improve Results*, London: Hodder and Stoughton.

McCormack, J., Propper, C. and Smith, S. (2013) *Herding Cats? Management and University Performance*, Centre for Market and Public Organisation, University of Bristol, Working Paper 13/308.

Watson, D. (2009) *The Question of Morale. Managing Happiness and Unhappiness in University Life*, Maidenhead: Open University Press.

▶ References

Bartlett, C. and Ghoshal, S. (1990) 'Matrix management: Not a structure, a frame of mind', *Harvard Business Review*, 68(4), 138–145.

Bolden, R., Gosling, J., O'Brien, A., Peters, K., Ryan, M. and Haslam, A. (2012) *Academic Leadership: Changing Conceptions, Identities and Experiences in UK Higher Education. Summary Report*, London: Leadership Foundation for Higher Education.

Deem, R. (1998) 'New managerialism in higher education – the management of performances and cultures in universities', *International Studies in the Sociology of Education,* 8(1), 47–70.

Kennie, T. (2009) Academic leadership: Dimensions, dysfunctions and dynamics, Ranmore Consulting Group, available at http://www.ranmore.co.uk/default. aspx, accessed 14 July 2013.

Larson, E. W. and Gobeli, D. H. (1987) 'Matrix management: Contradictions and insights', *California Management Review*, XXIX(4), 1–16.

Matthews, H., Brown, G., Furey-King, B. and Lloyd, M. (2006) *What Is It You Do Again? A Guide to Departmental Administration*, Manchester: AUA.

McCaffery, P. (2004) *The HE Manager's Handbook: Effective Leadership and Management in Universities and Colleges*, Abingdon: RoutledgeFalmer.

Temple, P. (2008) 'The integrative university: Why university management is different', *Perspectives: Policy and Practice in Higher Education*, 12(4), 99–102.

Watson, D. (2000) *Managing Strategy*, Buckingham: Open University Press.

Watson, D. (2012) 'Who runs universities?', *Perspectives: Policy and Practice in Higher Education*, 16(2), 41–45.

6 Mentoring and Coaching

Introduction

In the previous chapter, we focussed on the role that 'good managers' can play in fostering your career. We now turn our attention to two other types of relationship that may be of use to you in different ways throughout your career, namely mentoring and coaching. A quick informal survey of the staff development pages of most British universities is likely to turn up at least some reference to mentoring and coaching, from short seminars that introduce managers to a range of techniques for use in their day-to-day interaction with staff to accredited programmes that prepare selected staff to become part of a home-grown network of on-campus mentors or coaches tasked with raising the performance of the institution as a whole.

The widespread acceptance of both mentoring and coaching as important tools for improving individuals' achievement levels can, in part at least, be understood as part of the wider trend to embrace private sector management practices to which we referred in Chapter 5. Let's not allow ourselves to get side-tracked by the rights and wrong of that. Instead, this chapter explores how accessing mentorship and coaching might be useful to you as you seek to manage your career in higher education administration, when such relationships might be most beneficial and how to make the most of them. The roles of mentor and coach as we are using them in this book can both be described as work-based 'helping activities' (Alexander and Renshaw, 2005, p. 105). Although mentorship and coaching have some things in common and, as in this chapter's title, are often presented as a 'pair', there are both conceptual and practical differences between them. So let's explore their key features separately, considering their relative benefits at different points in your career.

▶ **Mentoring**

In one sense, of course, mentorship is nothing new. The modern idea of the 'mentor' can be traced back to Homer's Odyssey, in which Mentor is an older man whom Odysseus asks to look after his son whilst he goes off to fight the Trojans. In fact, Mentor himself is no great shakes; it is Athene, disguising herself as Mentor, who guides and advises Odysseus's son until his father returns. However, the association of Mentor with wise counsel has stuck, although today we are more likely to understand the terms 'mentor' and 'mentoring' in terms of sharing professional expertise.

Key forms of mentoring

In its purest form, mentoring can be described as a process whereby a person who is more senior in an organisation provides advice and guidance for someone less senior. That could, of course, sound like a description of line management. However, whilst a good line manager should be both advising and guiding their staff, mentoring is a non-hierarchical relationship and takes place outside of any line management structure. Mentoring relationships can be either formal or informal. Informal mentoring is when a relationship between a more and a less experienced member of staff grows up organically, for example, through networking opportunities. Formal relationships are ones that are positively fostered by the organisation, perhaps by making them a requirement at certain career stages (e.g. probation) or via a workplace mentoring scheme through which staff seeking mentorship are matched to staff who have volunteered to be mentors. These formal relationships tend to be of a shorter timescale and are often for a specific purpose, whereas informal relationships may well run over a longer timescale and have a wider remit.

In higher education today, the term 'mentoring' typically encompasses a wide range of relationships, some of which may be more relevant at particular stages in an individual's career. Tjan (2011) has identified three models of mentoring across a career: buddy/peer mentoring, career mentoring and life mentoring.

Buddy/peer mentoring

Buddy mentoring, which is very common in universities, occurs when someone new to the organisation or department is paired up with a colleague who 'knows the ropes' and can provide socialisation and induction functions; this person is often a peer rather than a more senior member of staff. Kirsten Gillingham highlights this:

> I was mentored as a Bursar when I came to Oxford – it wasn't formal mentoring, it was just having a 'buddy' actually. You were put in touch with another Bursar and they were there on the end of

a phone or invited you round for lunch or dinner a couple of times just to check you were getting on OK.

Such support can be invaluable when you are new to an organisation, providing a 'safe' contact to ask all those questions that you are afraid might be bit silly (but usually aren't).

Career mentoring

Career mentoring, by contrast, is rarely offered a matter of course, but can be particularly useful at those points when you want to start thinking about your next step, that is, career planning. If, like so many of us, you find yourself in a career in higher education administration somewhat by chance, this may well sound a bit too organised and ambitious! However, even if you are one of the many 'accidental' administrators, universities provide an environment that is both supportive and intellectually challenging in equal measure. To maximise your chances of building a successful career, whatever that means for you, you really should take career planning more seriously. And part of that, we'd suggest, should include seeking advice from career mentors. These mentors will not and should not remain the same: the literature suggests that our career opportunities are maximised by working with a variety of different mentors over time (and there is some evidence to suggest that this is especially so for women (Kay and Wallace, 2009)).

Tania Rhodes-Taylor highlights the benefits of informal mentoring:

> There's a member of Council that I'm working with at the moment who's a senior figure for a major international company and a graduate from here. I suspect if you spoke to him he'd say he was mentoring me, he's certainly helping me and assisting me ... Maybe that is mentoring but it's never been called it, but it's not about my professional development or the next stage of my career, it's more about 'we need to develop and get it through and implement it' and I'm using some of his expertise to support that. But then I've been bringing him up to speed on changes to the sector and current higher education issues because he's new on Council.

If the above indicates that different stages of your career will require different types of mentoring, it's also true that different aspects of any mentoring relationship may be more useful at different times. Kram (1983) has suggested that mentors can provide both career development and psychosocial development benefits. Career development functions include sponsorship, coaching, protection, exposure-and-visibility and challenging work assignments, whilst psychosocial functions include role modelling, acceptance-and-confirmation, counselling and friendship. Career development functions often depend on the mentor's power and position in the organisation, whereas the psychosocial function depends on the quality of the interpersonal relationship.

Tracy Carlton shares how she has used different mentors in her career:

> I have different experiences of mentoring, some have been my choice and some have been suggested through our career appraisal programme; the ones I have chosen myself have either been through consultants or trainers that we have used. One of the mentors I used was a neuro-linguistic programmer. I wanted him from a 'how do I engage even better with individuals' perspective, especially from a commercial environment. That was really helpful and one I initiated. The last one came through a contact of a contact, which was more driven as line management development for me. I think a mentor has to be on a personal level with personal values because, if you don't connect, they are going to force you down a route that you may not necessarily be comfortable with. In total I've used three types of mentor: one around commercial acumen, one around stakeholders and one around the technical skills.

Life mentoring

Tjan's final category is that of life mentors ad he suggests these may be the most important mentors to have. They can be people inside your institution, but also from outside. As you reach the mid- and senior stages of your careers, we often need to have someone in whom we can confide without feeling that there is any bias. This is someone who can be a periodic sounding board when one is faced with a difficult career challenge, or when considering changing jobs.

Benefits of mentoring

A number of studies have suggested that informal mentoring relationships are more effective than formal relationships for mentees. For example, Ragins and Cotton (1999) showed that mentees with informal mentors received more career development and psychosocial functions and had greater overall satisfaction than those with formal relationships (see Case Study 6.1 as an example of this). They also found that both formal and informal mentoring relationships provided increased earnings compared with staff with no history of being mentored; however mentees with a history of informal mentors reported earning significantly more than those with formal mentors. Chao et al. (1992) found that mentees with informal mentors received slightly more career development support, which might be due to the unique interplay between mentor and mentee and the fact that many informal relationships are based upon perceived interpersonal similarities and comfort (Ragins and Cotton, 1999).

That said, many organisations have set up formal mentoring schemes to try to replicate the perceived success of informal relationships, especially to provide additional support to women and other minority staff who are still under-represented in senior management positions (Murrell et al., 2008) and contrasting research by Pennington (2004) has indicated that mentoring is more effective when formalised and when the expectations and commitments of participants are made clear.

Case study 6.1: Michelle Gander, Head of University Secretary's Office, The Open University

Michelle Gander's experience of mentorship should convince us to be alert to opportunities at all times:

> One experience that I always share to get others thinking about this subject was when I applied and was interviewed for a job which I didn't get – I was disappointed but not surprised, as this was my first attempt at apply for a post at the next grade up. The amazing thing that happened was that a member of the interview panel contacted me afterwards and asked if I'd like her to mentor me. Wow, amazing, someone taking the time to think about what they could do to help someone achieve their goal and to offer to invest their time and energy! Perhaps you can see why this has stuck with me?

> We had a very constructive mentoring relationship for about eight months in which she really challenged my thinking and helped me to become reflective and to put in place some actions to help me achieve my aim. I thanked her for this recently when we met at a conference – she had forgotten how it had started but I had not. This small example shows what an effect a good mentor can have on someone.

So, the literature is unclear as to whether informal or formal schemes are more effective for the individual and calls into question the effectiveness of both the informal and formal mentoring schemes to provide positive outcomes in career and psychosocial development functions. Amanda Wilcox says:

> I have been asked to be a mentor a number of times. It can be an extremely valuable experience for both the mentee and the mentor. Success is often down to the interaction between the two parties – and personalities play a part here – it is important to match individuals carefully.

However, the differences reported in the effectiveness between informal and formal mentoring relationships may be too simplistic to capture the nuances of interpersonal relationships, such as the perceived quality of the mentoring relationship and Ragins et al. (2000) and Carnell et al. (2006) reported that dysfunctional relationships have more of a negative effect on the mentee than those staff who are not mentored.

What is an effective mentor?

Rather than working to a fixed agenda, the focus of a mentoring relationship is on those issues and concerns which arise from the mentee's day-to-day practice and about which the mentee feels a need to consult. Whilst mentoring arrangements may be formalised in certain instances, the process actually works best when there is also a degree of informality, with the mentor acting as a friend and colleague who can be relied on for advice and support, as and when the need arises. An effective mentor is regarded by colleagues as a highly competent member of staff in terms of both knowledge and of expertise, has good interpersonal skills including sensitive questioning skills, can listen and respond thoughtfully and flexibly and is adept at motivating, encouraging and giving feedback. A good mentor is also willing to be responsible for helping with someone else's professional development, is enthusiastic about the potential benefits of mentoring to mentees and is ready to commit the time and effort required to make a success of the mentoring relationship.

Amanda Wilcox, on this, says:

> Having a mentor can be invaluable. However, mentoring can be difficult, and it is never a good idea to impose a particular mentor on somebody. People often find their own natural mentors, and I'm an

advocate of that approach. I've had some excellent mentors since I've been at Hull, both internally and externally, people with whom I find it really valuable to just externalise and share things with.

Research suggests that the gender composition of the mentoring pair is a critical factor to the outcomes of the relationship with same-sex pairing seeming to be more beneficial for psychosocial functions than career development functions but with women benefiting from enhanced career development functions if the mentor is male. This, it has been proposed, is a function of power: males tend to hold senior positions within organisations with positional power and as such are better able to provide functions such as sponsorship, protection, exposure and challenging work assignments.

This view is supported by a number of studies that have found that mentees with male mentors received greater career development outcomes, for example increased earnings, than mentees with female mentors (Ragins and Cotton, 1999). However, Sosik and Godshalk (2000) and Carnell et al. (2006) found that same-sex/race and cross-sex/race mentoring relationships did not have any significant difference on the number of mentoring functions received. Ramaswami et al. (2010) suggested that the diverse outcomes of previous same-gender versus cross-gender mentoring relationship research on the tangible benefits to women may need to take into account the organisational culture. As a result, they concluded, women working in male-dominated organisational cultures should ensure that they are mentored by high ranking male staff who can use their power to provide development opportunities and introduce the mentee to their networks.

▶ Hints and tips for successful mentoring relationships

So, how can you make the most of any mentoring relationship?

Instruction versus construction

Latest thinking about the best ways to support students to learn tells us that the instruction model (i.e. sitting in lectures and being talked at) is one of the least effective methods for 'deep' learning to take place. Why then if we are being mentored would we want a mentor who takes that sort of approach? Mentors do fall into this trap – they give advice, they do most of the talking, and they are pleased to be seen as the expert. However, we know that learning takes place when both parties – in this instance, the mentor and mentee – enter into dialogue to reach a joint understanding. As such, the mentor should focus on the collaborative building of knowledge, will value the process as well as any outcomes and will learn with the mentee. Indeed, a study by Pennington in 2004 (Carnell et al., 2006) found that senior managers in higher education learn most effectively when

- high levels of challenge coexist with personal support;
- individual learning is integrated with group and organisational learning;
- an appropriate balance is struck between knowledge/understanding and reflection and action;
- a variety of formal and informal means are used to promote learning.

Of course, this is far more time consuming for the mentor and involves them really engaging, on a deep level, with their mentee – and this is why the personal relationship is so important. If you find yourself with a mentor with whom, for whatever reason, you do not 'click', it is far better to walk away than persist: destructive relationships are more damaging to individuals than no mentoring at all.

The process

One of the most important activities to undertake when you first meet your mentee/mentor is to ensure that you both have a clear understanding of what the purpose of the meetings is and to set some 'ground rules'. Both roles should be outlined and the mentor especially should make it clear at the start that they are not there simply to give the mentee all the answers and that it is about a process of discovery and learning. Other practical things are:

- Once the relationship has been agreed in whatever form, the mentor should contact the mentee to introduce themselves and to set a date for the first meeting.
- The importance of confidentiality on both sides should be stressed.
- At the first meeting, the mentee should be encouraged to think about the outcomes and a focus for the meetings.
- Both parties should keep in regular contact.
- Both parties should be clear about professional boundaries: these are organisational relationships that usually involve colleagues are different levels within the hierarchy.
- The mentee should send the mentor a loose agenda well before the meeting and should also follow up after each meeting by indicating what tasks they will complete and by when (if appropriate).

- Meetings should keep to time – both people's availability is limited and it is difficult to stop someone in full flow if the duration of any meeting hasn't been agreed in advance.
- Set a series of dates for a period, then review to see if you need to continue or can finish the formal relationship.

Being strategic

As you can see there is much to recommend mentoring to individual staff at whatever stage they are in their careers both as a mentee and as a mentor. However, it's important to be both flexible and strategic about your mentorship choices. Indeed, research suggests that you should, in particular:

- Have a variety of different mentors throughout your career.
- Look for mentors who can help you with career planning, as well as those who can help with the day job.
- Given that higher education remains male-dominated at the top, if possible, and especially when you reach middle management, try to find a senior male manager to mentor you.
- Recognise that informal mentoring that develops spontaneously can often be more effective than formal mentoring executed without real commitment.
- Ensure you are matched with a mentor who can provide support, advice and guidance where you need support at that time.
- Find a mentor outside your unit.
- Choose a mentor who can also act as a role model, if possible.
- Do not be afraid to stop the relationship if it is not working. Not everyone clicks – move on and find someone else.
- Discuss ground rules at the first meeting – there are many resources online.
- Know what you want to discuss with your mentor at each session (Gander, 2013).

Indeed, as one participant in the research that generated that list noted: 'the effect [of mentoring] was to give me confidence... [it's] difficult to overestimate the positive impact that this authentic approach to the mentoring role had on my motivation and confidence' (Personal correspondence with author, 2008).

▶ Coaching

So, there you have it: mentorship is not simply sitting back and having someone tell you what to do. As if we'd promote such anything so passive! And you can put any associations of coaching with angry men in tracksuits, blowing whistles and yelling at you to 'feel the burn' of out of your head too, certainly as far as career management is concerned. Google the term and you'll find a vast array of individuals, companies and accrediting bodies offering services and courses and promoting numerous different approaches to coaching: executive coaching, leadership coaching, life coaching, career coaching, business coaching, performance coaching, skills coaching, neurolinguistic programming (NLP)-based coaching, manager-as-coach…the list goes on. Behind the scenes, there is an interesting case study here on how new 'professions' emerge, shape themselves and receive external recognition that, amongst other things, highlights the continuing role that universities play in validating and legitimising knowledge (Moyes, 2013). However, that's a discussion for another day.

Coaching in the workplace

Coaching has only really gained a foothold in the workplace within the last two decades (Whitmore, 2009), even more recently within universities (Vitae, 2011). As you might expect, in its earliest incarnations, coaching was focussed largely on 'top management', hence the prominence of 'executive' and 'leadership' coaching in any web search. But it's by no means still limited to the privileged few. In fact, according to the Chartered Institute of Personnel and Development (2011), coaching is now firmly established within the arsenal of most British staff development programmes. Indeed, their most recent survey on the subject found some 77% of organisations consulted made use of coaching in the workplace. Moreover, of those, 84% were increasing coaching-related expenditure despite the prevailing straitened economic conditions.

Although no comparable survey currently exists for British universities, there is plenty of anecdotal evidence to suggest that coaching is becoming established in this sector too. We referred earlier to the existence of coaching schemes within a number of institutions, links to some examples of which are provided at the end of the chapter, as well to various internal short courses on coaching techniques. We can also point to a range of sector-wide initiatives; for example, recent work to consider the place of coaching within the career development of contract researchers (Vitae, 2011). Coaching also features strongly in the portfolio of the UK's Leadership Foundation for Higher Education (LFHE, undated) and is promoted by many relevant professional bodies (see, for example, UHR, undated). Certainly, most of the individuals we interviewed for this book had had some experience of either being coached or using coaching techniques with their own staff.

This is interesting because, for all the claims that the coaching 'industry' makes and its increasing status as an 'organisational aspirin'

(CIPD, 2012, p. 4), the evidence base from which to justify its popularity is fairly limited. Sure, there are plenty of books and articles on the how and what of coaching, as well as several professional bodies vying to take responsibility for validating the body of knowledge that underpins the coaching 'profession' (Grimley, 2013). But, as a recent review of the evidence for the effectiveness of coaching on business performance noted, much of the research is 'advocacy, rather than enquiry', focusses on theoretical disputes between different 'schools of coaching' and relies on case studies, rather than utilising the kinds of randomised control trials or metrics-based evaluations from which it might be possible to draw generalisable conclusions (CIPD, 2012; see also Grimley, 2013; Vitae, 2011). This is not to say that coaching is therefore quackery and that you can skip to the next chapter. It's just important to recognise that at least some of its popularity currently derives from individuals' positive 'lived experiences', rather than from empirical research.

So why would universities invest in coaching? According to the CIPD study we mentioned above, the most common reasons reported by employers in general were to aid leadership development (61%), to build on good performance (48%), to improve employee skills and capability (47%) and to improve poor performance (43%). In other words, it's about achieving success by raising the performance of individuals – be that in an aspirational or remedial sense. This, Hugh Jones suggests, is particularly important in sectors like higher education:

> [I]ncreasingly I think university administration is knowledge work in the sense that we have to define the problem as well as shape the answer. So the olden days of fixed roles and fixed things to do and an obvious path are gone, completely gone. Universities have to be more dynamic and they have to behave like businesses, while not being businesses, and that means a lot of the role of the university administration is to create that possibility. Therefore defining your own job and the problem you're trying to deal with matters, and that's quite daunting. Sometimes you need to talk to someone about that who isn't your boss and who doesn't report to you. Because there are things you can't say to those people! It's often the case that you do, in fact, know the answer, you just don't know that you know it.

What coaching can do, then, is to give you new insights into the way you are at work (and in life more generally): how you respond to different situations, people and environments and why; what might be getting in the way of you achieving your goals and indeed, what your goals really are. Whether that's about an immediate 'thorny' issue or longer-term ambitions, advocates of coaching enthuse about its transformative powers for individuals, as well as for organisations as a whole. Particular benefits for individuals include increased self-awareness or 'mindfulness', enhanced problem solving skills, greater resilience and flexibility and increased self-confidence in their ability to do things well. Coaching, as Case Study 6.2 demonstrates, provides a way through the muddle.

Case study 6.2: Tessa Harrison, Registrar, University of Southampton

Tessa Harrison spoke of the powerful impact of coaching on her leadership style:

> [We] basically looked at my competencies and compared those to the competencies of a huge number of leaders, senior leaders in all sorts of different industries and what came through was that I needed to rebalance the time I was spending on thinking and strategizing against the time I spent on doing.

> So if you looked at my diary when I first started [...] it was just literally from eight o'clock in the morning until six o'clock at night at meetings, no lunch, nothing, just bang, bang, bang, bang. That's not a leader, a leader doesn't have back to back meetings. That's a manager, that's someone who's making things work. So there were issues in there about delegation, about control, stepping up to senior leadership, all of those things.

Whilst the coaching represents a real investment on the University's part in her leadership skills, the process itself has not been easy:

> It is very tough. I feel the University wants me to succeed and is giving me the support to succeed, which is wonderful [...] but it's tough and good coaching should be tough.

▶ How does coaching work?

As we'll see below, the commonplace pairing of coaching with mentoring is not without justification; certainly, a good portion of the advice on mentoring above can be applied without too much difficulty to coaching. What distinguishes coaching from mentoring is the purpose of the relationship between the two parties: whilst the mentor's role is to share their wisdom and knowledge to the mentee, be that in terms of how an organisation works, how to deal with a particular issue or how future career aspirations might be made real, the role of the coach is to provide a 'contained space' (Western, 2006, p. 34) within which the coachee can think creatively and generate their own solutions though listening, questioning and reflecting back.

Coaching, fundamentally, is about stimulating and supporting an individual to recognise and realise their own potential. Critically, the coach's views are not material to the discussion; rather the focus must be on the coachee finding their own way forward and part of that process must include feeling able to explore any avenue without fear of censure or judgement from the coach. That doesn't mean that a coach won't provide feedback or challenge the coachee's assumptions. Quite the contrary: it is essential that coaches don't collude with their coachee in avoiding difficult or uncomfortable issues. Challenge should be robust and coaching sessions can be emotionally charged. But the coachee should not feel under attack and so questioning should be couched in non-judgemental terms – such as 'what would happen if...' rather than 'why don't you...' and verbs like 'could' and 'might' instead of 'should' and 'must' (Alexander and Renshaw, 2005, pp. 122–127; Whitmore, 2009, p. 52).

It should also be non-directive: whilst the coach might propose different exercises to help the coachee organise and analyse their thinking, they must also let the coachee follow their own train of thought and explore ideas that they have generated themselves. And how is this different from therapy, you might well ask? Certainly, some of the skills and techniques used by coaches, counsellors and psychotherapists are similar, in particular active listening and action-orientation. The key difference is that coaching assumes that the client is fundamentally 'resourceful, creative and whole' and as such 'does not seek to analyse and resolve any underlying psychosocial pathology' (Vitae, 2011, p. 9; see also Grimley, 2013).

That doesn't mean that every kind of situation is 'coachable'. If the building is on fire, being asked to reflect upon how that makes you feel may not be very helpful. Likewise, there will be times when what you really do want is advice from a more experienced colleague or simply a clear instruction as to what needs to be done. And as far as the day job is concerned, your line manager will have something to say about what you do and how you do it! Coaching is one of an array of tools, not a cult.

▶ Accessing coaching in a university context

Within universities, there are several ways through which you might access coaching, with varying degrees of formality.

Professional/external coaching

At one end of the scale is 'professional' coaching, normally delivered by someone external to the organisation hired specifically for that purpose. They may be engaged by an employer or by an individual and may have little or no knowledge of the particular sector in which their coachee is working. They remain outside of the organisation, share no relationship with the coachee except through the coaching exchange and have no direct interest in defining the outcome of the coaching exchange. It may be tempting, therefore, to regard external coaching as the gold standard. Certainly, there is some evidence to suggest that those coached externally report greater satisfaction with the process than those coached internally. In part, this may be due to a perceived greater credibility and expertise with 'professional' coaches (Sue-Chan and Latham, 2004); however, Paul Greatrix explains the benefits thus:

> The most effective thing is actually just being able to talk to someone outside the University about the problems I face and how to deal with them – the strategies for dealing with difficult stuff that I'm not able to talk about with anyone inside the University and, indeed, if I were to talk to someone – peers – at another university, [...] it wouldn't be right. It's also the kind of thing you can't take home either. It's someone that does actually understand where I am at, but is able to reflect it back and give me an opportunity to be completely open and help me work out a way forward.

So confidentiality and the freedom to be open that comes with it are important. However, it is worth remembering that behind that 'helping activity' there is a financial transaction, potentially a fairly significant one at that, and an expectation of a positive outcome. If it's the employer who is paying, they will have an interest in the outcome. They may have initiated the coaching in response to a specific concern they have about some aspect of your work, as was the case with one of our interviewees, or because they see something in you that could be developed further. Either way, don't panic: if you were a dead-loss, they'd probably be looking at other options! It's just important to bear in mind that, whilst the detailed content of the exchange itself should always be confidential, the coach will still be answerable to the employer in some way, so you need to understand the extent to which they might be expected to report back on you (see the subsequent section on practical matters) and also to think carefully about whether you are going to be able to be open and honest with the coach if issues arise that concern those who have commissioned the coaching for you.

For this reason, Hugh Jones suggests that there may be times when it's worth paying for coaching yourself, 'because then they are only accountable to you, not the university. And it's your coach'. Whether that is a realistic option for you will depend on your own personal resources. Similarly, the option of accessing a professional coach through your employer may be a function of your relative career stage and/or the nature of any coaching programmes your institution may offer. However, if it's not an option, don't despair, because there is evidence to suggest that the majority of coaching is delivered not by external contractors, but by employees themselves.

Internal or peer coaching

According to CIPD figures from 2011, external coaches, although on the increase, account for only 20% of those delivering coaching in workplace settings; by far the most important sources of coaching are line managers (32%), followed by 'internal coaches' (23%). And both these models are increasingly accessible within the higher education sector, certainly as far as the UK is concerned. Internal coaches in the CIPD's definition included professional coaches who were on the payroll, as well as volunteers who had undergone specific training. We've already noted that internal coaching schemes are increasingly common within British universities. So how do they work?

The programme at the University of York is typical: coaches are volunteers and undertake a specific accredited programme. Access to these 'peer' coaches is coordinated through the scheme and is open to all staff, subject to an application process and, normally, the support of the line manager. The purpose and objectives of coaching are agreed between the coachee and line manager. As such, whilst the content of sessions remains confidential between the coach and coachee, the coachee is expected to update the line manager on progress towards the agreed objectives and how they will apply their learning in the workplace. Coaching sessions take place every four to eight weeks, are around 60–90 minutes long and normally take place during working hours. Whilst there is no specific limit on the coaching relationship's duration, its effectiveness and impact are evaluated periodically, with input from the line manager as well as the coach and coachee (University of York, 2011). The programme is clearly outcomes-oriented and highlights its anticipated benefits for individuals, team and the wider institution, giving an insight into why employers might be prepared to invest time and money in coaching.

The challenge for both coach and coachee in models such as this is in achieving the necessary levels of trust, openness and rapport required for coaching to be really effective. The input of the line manager may limit the coachee's capacity to explore certain issues or their willingness to share their real views and concerns. At the same time, the knowledge that both parties have of the organisation and how it operates may compromise the coach's capacity to maintain the necessary disinterestedness and neutrality. It may also impede effective communication if each is making assumptions about what the other knows and feels. Good training and ongoing 'supervision' of coaches (by which is meant providing coaches with opportunities to discuss their practice with each other) can help in addressing some of these issues (Connor and Pokora, 2012; Zenger and Stinnett, 2006). Likewise, ensuring that coachees understand and commit to the coaching process is important. In any case, confidentiality notwithstanding, internal coaching networks can raise mutual understanding across an organisation by bringing into contact colleagues who might otherwise understand little of each other's worlds (Ideus, 2005). If you can find the right internal coach, then, there is every prospect of achieving the same kinds of benefits as might be available from an external, 'professional' coach.

Coaching by line managers

Given what we've said previously about the need for coaches to maintain distance, remain neutral and avoid instructing the coachee, the notion that line managers can be effective coaches of their staff may seem a strange one. Yet there is a rich seam of literature to explore that advocates the idea of the 'line manager as coach' (Alexander and Renshaw, 2005; Starr, 2008; Whitmore, 2009). Likewise, the CIPD data referred to above and the anecdotal evidence from university staff development websites suggest an increasing expectation that line managers should be trained in coaching techniques. Just how realistic is the line manager as coach?

In theory, it's possible. For advocates like Whitmore, the skills of the coach are the skills of a good line manager, the ability to get employees to take responsibility for their work combining with deeper listening to the challenges they face, thereby enabling the line manager to maintain control and achieve success (2009, p. 24). Others, however, have pointed to tensions between the day-to-day responsibilities of line managers around work allocation and performance review on the one hand and the requirement to stand back that is so core to coaching on the other, as well as real time pressures, power differentials and possible personality traits that make it difficult for both line managers and their staff to switch easily into the roles of coach and coachee – and back again. As such, Anderson et al. argue:

The role of 'manager as coach' is more effectively articulated as one of 'management style' that is characterised by: regular coaching conversations; effective feedback processes; the encouragement of superior performance; and the development of productive and trusting relationships in the workplace.   (2009, p. 12)

Importantly, they also suggest that line managers find the adoption of a coaching style easier the more senior they are, which, they argue, may be a result of their more limited responsibility for day-to-day operational decision-making. The lesson here is to be realistic about the extent to which your line manager can also be your coach: it's fair to expect them to let you come up with ideas and contribute to how things are done; but don't expect them necessarily to be able to give you the time, attention and autonomy to set goals that comes as standard with more formal professional and peer coaching arrangements. Kirsten Gillingham's description of coaching her staff may be helpful here:

[It is] defining particular challenges, identifying with them what steps they could take and encouraging them to go and find their own solutions – go and research this, go and have a look at that, go and talk to so-and-so and see what you can find out and what you want to try to do. Then coming back and looking at how that worked and reflecting on it and then challenging them on the next thing to think about the next thing to do, so it was kind of a process of trying to get them to find their own way through things but helping them with that, and making that space for reflection, to talk about 'what did that do' and 'how did that work'.

▶ Making coaching work for you

Whatever type of coaching you access and for whatever reason, it's important to know what to expect from your coach and what is expected from you.

Choosing your coach
Assuming you have some say in who your coach is – and really, unless it's your line manager, you should expect to have a say – here are some key things to look for:

- What credentials does the coach have? Have they undergone any formal training for example, and do they belong to a professional body? Do they come from a particular school of thought? This is important because of the potential for coaching to stray beyond the purely professional and into the personal and emotional spheres (Grimley, 2013);

- How will they access supervision and are you comfortable with that? Particularly for internal coaches, you might want to know who they might discuss their practice with. Even though they will be bound to maintain confidentiality, depending on the issues you raise, you may worry about being identifiable within the institution.

- How and where are you going to interact with them? Particularly with external coaches, questions of venue and mode of communication may arise. Do you want to have face-to-face meetings or might telephone-based coaching be an option you could consider? If the latter, how are you going to make sure you protect that time and have the necessary privacy? If face-to-face is your preference, how are you going to achieve it?

- Do you trust them? Again, critical: if you are not convinced of their integrity, there is a danger that you will keep things back and so fail to make real progress;

- Do you like them? This is important: feeling able to talk freely is essential.

If the answer to these last two questions is no, then, as with mentoring, it's best to look elsewhere. If it's yes, the next step should be 'contracting', by which we mean agreeing explicitly how the coaching relationship will work. There is general agreement in the practitioner literature that this is essential, whether or not the relationship involves a direct financial transaction or not. As such, it should cover both practical matters – when and where; duration; ways of working – as well as initial goals, expectations on both sides, any boundaries and limits to discussions, reporting requirements and how the effectiveness of the relationship will be reviewed (Connor and Pokora, 2012). It's also worth making sure that any acronyms are mutually understood: coaching theory is awash with them – but then so is higher education. Taking the time to clarify these matters – and to revisit them as necessary – is worth it, even if it means that you can't get stuck in to the coaching process immediately. Any coach worthy of that title should not let you miss the contracting stage.

Being a good coachee

Since coaching is focussed so much on you, your needs and your solutions to them, it almost goes without saying that you need to commit to the process for it to work. Obviously that includes your time – both during sessions and also between them, because the chances are you'll have 'homework', whether that's undertaking a particular exercise on paper or implementing real-time actions to see what happens. Additionally, you need to be prepared for a bumpy ride: coaching can be tough and, whilst its primary focus is future-facing, it's possible that you will find yourself looking back into your past to account for the way you react today or facing up to some tough facts about the reality of your current situation vis-à-vis your aspirational one. So you might feel very exposed and defensive at times, angry and dejected at others. This is a normal part of the coaching process (Whitmore, 2009); it's tough, but recognising that coaching is not a quick fix is important. Lastly, you do need to be honest – with your coach but most importantly with yourself. A coaching exchange is not the place for posturing or presenting your best self: don't go looking for a coach who can directly assist you with your career. That's what networking is for – and, at times, mentorship. Remember, the critical difference between coaching and mentoring is that the coach remains detached. Use the coaching session as a safe space in which to work out what you want to do. Then do it in the 'real world'!

▶ Conclusion

In this chapter we've explored two tools that can, at different times in your career, be particularly helpful in enabling you to manage your career effectively. Mentorship, with its focus on learning from the experience and expertise of others, can be a powerful means by which to extend and grow your understanding of the sector and the opportunities and challenges it presents, as well as broadening your networks. Coaching, by contrast, is about understanding yourself, how you behave and react, what that means for your current performance, goals and future aspirations and what you are going to do about it. Both have credibility within the sector and so you should spend some time thinking about how and when they might be valuable to you – and perhaps also to those you manage. The next chapter, in which we look at some of the 'big' decisions that you might face over the trajectory of your career, may well provide you with some food for thought.

▶ Further reading

Links to a small selection of university-based coaching and/or mentoring schemes across the UK:

University of Aberdeen: http://www.abdn.ac.uk/staffnet/working-here/coaching-and-mentoring.php

University of East Anglia: http://www.uea.ac.uk/csed/coaching

University of Warwick:
   http://www2.warwick.ac.uk/services/ldc/coachmentor/wcm/

University of York: https://www.york.ac.uk/admin/hr/coaching/

References

Alexander, G. and Renshaw, B. (2005) *Supercoaching: The Missing Ingredient for High Performance*, London: Random House Business Books.

Anderson, V., Rayner, C. and Schyns, B. (2009) *Coaching at the Sharp End: The Role of Line Managers in Coaching at Work*, London: Chartered Institute of Personnel and Development.

Carnell, E., MacDonald, J. and Askew, S. (2006) *Coaching and Mentoring in Higher Education*, London: Institute of Education.

Chao, G. T., Walz, P. M. and Gardner, P. D. (1992) 'Formal and informal mentorships: A comparison on mentoring functions and contrast with non-mentored counterparts', *Personnel Psychology*, 45, 619–636.

CIPD (2011) *The Coaching Climate*, London: Chartered Institute of Personnel and Development.

CIPD (2012) *Coaching: The Evidence*, London: Chartered Institute of Personnel and Development.

Connor, M. and Pokora, J. (2012) *Coaching and Mentoring at Work: Developing Effective Practice*, Maidenhead: Open University Press.

Gander, M. A. (2013) 'The effect of a formal career mentoring scheme on women administrators, or, what mentoring can do for you', *Perspectives: Policy and Practice in Higher Education*, 17(2), 71–75.

Grimley, B. (2013) *Theory and Practice of NLP Coaching: A Psychological Approach*, London: Sage.

Ideus, K. (2005) 'The leader as coach', *Industrial and Commercial Training*, 37(4), 189–192.

Kay, F. M. and Wallace, J. E. (2009) 'Mentors as social capital: Gender, mentors, and career rewards in law practice', *Sociological Inquiry*, 79(4), 418–452.

Kram, K. E. (1983) 'Phases of the mentor relationship', *Academy of Management Journal*, 26(4), 608–625.

LFHE (undated) Coaching, http://www.lfhe.ac.uk/en/consultancy-coaching/coaching/index.cfm, accessed 23 August 2013.

Moyes, H. (2013) 'Book review: Theory and practice of NLP coaching', *Perspectives: Policy and Practice in Higher Education*, published online 14 August 2013.

Murrell, A. J., Blake-Beard, S., Porter, D. M. and Perkins-Williamson, A. (2008) 'Interorganizational formal mentoring: Breaking the concrete ceiling sometimes requires support from the outside', *Human Resource Management*, 47(2), 275–294.

Ragins, B. R. and Cotton, J. L. (1999) 'Mentor functions and outcomes: A comparison of men and women in formal and informal mentoring relationships', *Journal of Applied Psychology*, 84(4), 529–550.

Ragins, B. R., Cotton, J. L. and Miller, J. S. (2000) 'Marginal mentoring: The effects of type of mentor, quality of relationships, and program design on work and career attitudes', *Academy of Management Journal*, 43(6), 1177–1194.

Ramaswami, A., Dreher, G. F., Bretz, R. and Wiethoff, C. (2010) 'Gender, mentoring, and career success: The importance of organizational context', *Personnel Psychology*, 63, 385–405.

Sosik, J. J. and Godshalk, V. M. (2000) 'The role of gender in mentoring: Implications for diversified and homogenous mentoring relationships', *Journal of Vocational Behavior*, 57, 102–122.

Starr, J. (2008) *Brilliant Coaching: How to Be a Brilliant Coach in Your Workplace*, Harlow: Pearson.

Sue-Chan, C. and Latham, G. P. (2004) 'The relative effectiveness of external, peer and self-coaches', *Applied Psychology: An International Review*, 53(2), 260–278.

Tjan, A. K. (2011) Keeping great people with three kinds of mentors, *Harvard Business Review*, http://blogs.hbr.org/tjan/2011/08/keeping-great-people-with-thre.html, accessed 12 April 2013.

UHR (undated) Coaching for HR directors, http://www.uhr.ac.uk/PageInfo.aspx?careers-22-Coaching.html, accessed 23 August 2013.

Vitae (2011) *Coaching for Research in UK Higher Education Institutions: A Review*, Cambridge: Careers Research and Advisory Centre Ltd.

Western, S. (2006) 'Look who's talking', *People Management*, January, 31–33.

Whitmore, J. (2009) *Coaching for Performance: Growing Human Potential and Purpose. The Principles and Practice of Coaching and Leadership*, London: Nicholas Barely.

Zenger, J. H. and Stinnett, K. (2006) 'Leadership coaching: Developing effective executives', *Chief Learning Officer*, July, 44–47.

7 Making Positive Career Choices

Introduction

So, armed with all the information from the previous chapters, we return to our original question: can you have a successful career in higher education administration? The resounding answer is yes; it is possible to plan a career and be successful, but you need to be proactive, take responsibility, seek opportunities and be prepared to pursue a career that covers both a breadth and a depth of experience. As Amanda Wilcox observes:

> It's useful to have had a variety of roles in higher education, even very junior ones. There are lots of administrative roles that people would be well qualified for as a graduate, in either academic or central administrative departments. Having some breadth for the first few years that you work in higher education will be an advantage to you. I think it's really useful if you can have that experience between working in different departments and faculties in an administrative role (they have very different flavours and the discipline of the faculty does make a difference to how the administration works) and working in the central university services.

In higher education institutions, we do have the possibility of being re-graded (i.e. having the salary banding of our job reviewed), although you need to bear in mind that it is jobs that are graded, rather than people, and that grades can go down, as well as up. So, whilst you can't plan for it, you could find yourself in a position where you progress up the salary scales because your job has changed, rather than because you've changed job. What it won't do it is give you any more skills and experience. It's great to have your efforts recognised, of course, but on the flip side you may not want to stay too long in one position. In any case, successful re-grading applications are not so common. In short, you should expect to progress by changing job.

▶ Defining career success

Let's take just a moment to stop and reflect on what career success means. As mentioned in Chapter 3, success can be seen as intrinsic, as in someone who is completely happy in their role and therefore what they gain from the role makes them successful in their own minds – what we commonly term 'job satisfaction'. As Sarah Randall-Paley says:

> I think it is important to consider what success and happiness mean and to recognise that your view of what this means may change over time. I think it's about being comfortable with yourself. You need to think about what you'd gain by moving job at any time.

Another measure of success is extrinsic, that is, that not only the job itself is rewarding to an individual, but that they are seen as being successful through their position and/or remuneration (Heslin, 2003; Powell and Mainiero, 1992). Heslin (2003) reports that five of the most common precursors of career success are gender, personality, education, mentoring relationships and career tactics. The first two are ascribed characteristics, with gender being a negative indicator for women for salary, managerial level and promotion. The personality traits of conscientiousness and extraversion have also both been associated with higher subsequent job satisfaction and income.

Skill requirements found to contribute to people's success were opportunities to develop general management skills, having challenging work assignments, development of line management skills, having a diverse range of work positions, networking with others, being politically savvy about interpersonal communication and having a good boss or mentor (Burke and Attridge, 2011; Lyness and Thompson, 2000). Of interest too is research by De Pater et al. (2010) which showed that women get fewer challenging work assignments than men when the data are controlled for ambition and socio-demographic variables.

Human capital determinants refer to the personal investment that individuals make to enrich their careers; and human capital theory posits that individuals' investments in education, training and work experience will increase their value on the labour market. This is something that we stressed in Chapter 3: we need to take responsibility as individuals for our career development and to invest some of our own time, energy and possibly money into helping ourselves achieve our goals; our institutions cannot be expected to pick up all of the cost of our development.

Tables 7.1–7.3 offer overview career maps showing how the three authors' careers have progressed to date alongside the additional training, development and other career-enhancing activities that have helped developed our careers. From these examples, you can see that all three of us have undertaken both professional development to help us in our current roles and prepare us for the next step (we are increasing our human capital), as well as undertaking other assignments (internal or external to the institution) on top of our jobs to increase our technical skills and broaden our general awareness (and sometimes just because it's interesting – or even fun).

There is a 'but' coming here: you can't do everything, you have to learn to say 'no' (constructively) and you also need to learn to prioritise. Being clear with yourself about what your priorities are at the current time will inform what additional activities you can take on. For example, you may be able to find time in your day to do some internal courses but it would be impossible to take on anything outside of your work day such as an MBA – at the moment. In a few years, things might well change. The key thing is that you need to define your own success and what's important to you, rather than what is important to other people. Continuously re-evaluating your priorities will allow you to view your career management rationally and make plans for what and when you do certain things.

▶ Careers in higher education administration

You don't have to follow the 'academic civil service' model, a linear trajectory from administrative assistant to assistant and senior assistant registrar posts, and onward to academic registrar and registrar (Whitchurch, 2009); although that route is available, it is arguably less common. Your challenge in today's institutions is to think about how you get to where you want to be when new jobs are being created that we haven't seen before or where gaining a broad range of experience will stand you in good stead. As Weiner argues, what we mean by 'career' is ripe for re-conceptualising, which she argues is particularly relevant for women: 'a winding or unstructured path might be a more accurate definition of career progress' (in Cuthbert, 1996, p. 67).

So, yes, you can make a career in higher education administration; and yes, there are many different pathways and definitions of success. In order to achieve the outcomes you desire, we recommend that you undertake career planning after reflecting on your current skills and experience and where you want to be next. The outcomes of the planning may be very specific – it could be about undertaking a sector-specific qualification to enhance your knowledge base or using

Table 7.1 Career map of Michelle Gander, Head of University Secretary's Office, The Open University

Role/grade	Length of time in post	Reason for leaving	Key skills/knowledge acquired	Professional development and other career-enhancing activities
Curriculum Manager (SP30–39), Faculty of Technology, The Open University	4 years	Promotion	• Project management • Communication skills • Working collaboratively with academics • Understanding of pedagogy • Budgeting • Website design for teaching online student support • Presentation skills	Internal courses: • Understanding budgets • Understanding copyright • Presentation skills • Communication skills • Negotiation skills Other activities: • Associate Lecturer for a number of Open University (OU) modules • Exam marker • Joined Association of University Administrators
Programme Manager (SP37–47), Faculty of Technology, The Open University	3 years	Sideways move	Enhanced all of above plus: • Programme management • Matrix management • Governance requirements • External horizon scanning/market intelligence	Internal courses: • Systems thinking • Dreamweaver • Influencing skills • Line management skills Other activities: • Effective recruitment • Project manager for institutional project • First career development mentor

Table 7.1 (Continued)

Role/grade	Length of time in post	Reason for leaving	Key skills/knowledge acquired	Professional development and other career-enhancing activities
Senior Manager, Curriculum and Qualifications (SP37–47), Strategy Unit, The Open University	14 months	Secondment	• Market intelligence • Student number planning • Resource allocation • Risk management • Institutional-level project management	Internal courses: • Microsoft project External courses: • Oxford Centre for Higher Education Policy Studies (OxCHEPS) summer school • Open University Postgraduate Certificate in Business Administration Other activities: • Member of Chartered Management Institute • School governor
Senior Faculty Administrator (SP45–51), Faculty of Health and Social Care, The Open University	4 years	Promotion	• Strategic finance • Line management • Strategic human resources • Management of significant budget reduction • Research management • Knowledge transfer	Internal courses: • Research methodologies module • Employment law External courses: • MBA in Higher Education Management, Institute of Education Other activities: • Non-Executive Director, British School of Osteopathy • Author of chapter in OU module reader • Awarded Chartered Manager • First publication in *Perspectives*

| Head of University Secretary's Office (senior pay scale), The Open University | Current | n/a | • Risk management
• Institutional governance
• Institutional strategy
• Academic regulations and qualification approval
• Equality and diversity
• Fees and funding in all UK nations
• Project director/senior accountable executive on institutional projects | External courses:
• Senior strategic leadership from the Leadership Foundation for Higher Education
• 'Practitioner' in risk management (M_o_R)
• 'Practitioner' in programme management (MSP)
• 'Foundation level' in change management

Other activities:
• Awarded Fellowship of Association of University Administrators
• Started blog on women in HE, management, etc.
• Wrote this book
• Second and third publications in *Perspectives* |

Table 7.2 Career map of Heather Moyes, Business Manager, Vice Chancellor's Office, Cardiff University

Role/grade	Time in post	Reason for leaving	Key skills/knowledge acquired	Professional development and other career-enhancing activities
Executive Officer: Postgraduate Research, (SP23–30), Research and Graduate College, University of Salford	15 months	Career progression	• HE policy • Communication skills • Working collaboratively with academics • Marketing and external relations • Presentation skills	Internal courses: • Committee servicing Other activities: • Joined Association of University Administrators • Undertook project for Internal Audit Committee on student representation • Attended UK Council for Graduate Education conference
Faculty Administrator: Social Sciences, (SP23–30), Academic Registry, Lancaster University	3 years, including period of maternity leave	Promotion	• Governance • Teaching quality • Research support • Working with regulatory bodies • Committee servicing • Project management • Needs of Arts and Social Sciences disciplines	Internal courses: • Various role-specific courses Other activities: • Partial secondment to support institutional project to develop new programme approval processes

Faculty Manager, (SP30–38), Faculty of Arts and Social Sciences, Lancaster University	3 years, including period of maternity leave	Relocation (following husband)	• People management • Change management • Financial management • Strategic planning and implementation • HE policy	Internal courses: • People management • Coaching and mentoring (Postgraduate Certificate) External courses: • Oxford Centre for Higher Education Policy Studies (OxCHEPS) summer school • Association of University Administrators' workshop on managing difficult people Other activities: • Attended Association of University Administrators' conference • Participated in peer action-learning set • Parenthood!

Table 7.2 (Continued)

Role/grade	Time in post	Reason for leaving	Key skills/knowledge acquired	Professional development and other career-enhancing activities
School Manager (SP38–45; then 45–51 following re-grade), School of Nursing and Midwifery, Cardiff University	5 years	Secondment	• Strategic finance • Business process review • Strategic human resources • External relations • Contract management • Knowledge transfer • Internationalisation • Understood needs of health-related disciplines • Involvement in institutional projects and working groups	Internal courses: • Lean processes • Facilitation skills External courses: • MBA in Higher Education Management, Institute of Education Other activities: • Ad hoc coaching and mentoring • Welsh Higher Education Administration conference • Association of University Administrators' conference ×2 • Speaker at conference on 'Lean' • Guest speaker on career development programme for women (ongoing) • Two different external mentors

Role	Duration	Reason	Skills/experience	Development activities
Project Manager (SP45–51), School of Chemistry, Cardiff University	11 months	End of secondment; new post (sideways move)	• Change management • Project management • Negotiation and persuasion • Financial management • Complex HR • Needs of natural science disciplines	Internal courses: • Sensitive conversations Other activities: • Wales Association of University Administrators' conference • Book review for *Perspectives* • Wrote this book • Involved in re-establishing local Association of University Administrators' branch • Received professional coaching • Became a charity trustee
Business Manager (SP45–51), Vice Chancellor's Office, Cardiff University	Current	n/a	• Institutional project support • Institutional strategy and implementation • Supporting senior leadership (Pro-VC) • HE policy • Complex portfolio management	Other activities: • Participated in Association of University Administrators' short-life working group on HE careers • Presented at Association of University Administrators' Development and Skills conference • Presented at Association of University Administrators' national conference

Table 7.3 Career map of Emma Sabzalieva, College Registrar, St Antony's College, University of Oxford

Role/grade	Length of time in post	Reason for leaving	Key skills/knowledge acquired	Professional development and other career-enhancing activities
Communications Office Manager (SP equivalent 16–22), Aga Khan Humanities Project (now part of University of Central Asia), Tajikistan	2 years (was a translator for just less than a year and then was promoted)	Fixed-term contract	• People management • Project management • Taking initiative • Developed language skills • Communication skills, particularly in international settings • Writing a strategic plan • Evaluation	External courses: • Certificate in Peace and Reconciliation Studies (Coventry University, distance learning) Other activities: • Various community outreach projects • Led communications and skills training in two languages • Organised international student conference and secured funding • Turned charity's library into open-access resource centre

| MA and Research Student Administrator (SP21–27), Institute of Education, University of London | 15 months | Promotion | • Course administration
• First experience of working in UK HE
• Coordinating a major EU research funding proposal
• Marketing/student recruitment
• Student recruitment
• Bespoke databases | Internal courses:
• Various courses, e.g. covering IT programmes
External courses:
• Postgraduate certificate in Conflict and Development, Open University
Other activities:
• Worked with colleagues in European universities to market new Erasmus Mundus Master's degree
• Improved process for coordinating doctoral vivas |
| Research and Consultancy Administrator (SP25–31), Institute of Education, University of London | 1 year | Relocation | • Preparing budgets for research bids
• Financial forecasting
• How university consultancies operate
• Briefing (orally/in writing) senior members of staff
• Facilitating international university partnerships | Internal courses:
• Various courses, e.g. on institution's research database
Other activities:
• Represented institution at research project meeting in Switzerland
• Parenting |

Table 7.3 (Continued)

Role/grade	Length of time in post	Reason for leaving	Key skills/knowledge acquired	Professional development and other career-enhancing activities
Scholarships and Exchanges Officer (SP29–36), University of Oxford	1 year	Promotion	• Donor relations and negotiation • Governance at Oxford (ongoing) • Budgeting • Developing good relationships with senior academics • Team restructuring and re-grading processes • Student complaints	Internal courses: • Various internal courses, e.g. negotiation Other activities: • Joined Association of University Administrators; member of International Higher Education Special Interest Group • Set up informal funding network with counterparts at Cambridge University
Head of Graduate Funding (SP37–43), University of Oxford	2 years 8 months	Career progression/diversification	• Financial control and management • Team development • Recruitment • Writing and presenting committee papers • Government (UK and international) HE funding policy • Legal requirements	External courses: • MBA in Higher Education Management, Institute of Education Other activities: • Set up online discussion group for MBA participants • Attended UK Council for Graduate Education conference • Deputised for colleague in Development Office

Role	Duration	Transition	Responsibilities	Development
Senior Tutor, Somerville College (SP42–47), University of Oxford	7 months	End of secondment	• HR functions – recruitment, personnel matters for academic and administrative staff • Writing and presenting policy papers • Initiating and overseeing a team restructure	External courses: • Finished MBA in Higher Education Management Other activities: • Participated in conference on doing research in former Soviet countries • Joined Society for Research into Higher Education (SRHE) • Introduced support programme for final-year students
Implementation Lead (Project Manager) (SP37–43), Student Systems Programme, University of Oxford	8 months	Sideways move	• System development • Convening and coordinating a university-wide steering group • Technology to support teaching and learning • Collaborative software (e.g. Sharepoint) • Mentoring a junior colleague from a different unit • Simultaneously worked on professional development of administrators project	Other activities: • Volunteer judge for Pan African Awards in Entrepreneurship in Education • School governor, member of finance sub-committee • Started blog on HE/social change in Central Asia • Independent research project on HE in Central Asia; paper presented at international multidisciplinary conference in Germany • Guest speaker on internal course on thinking about management • Presented at Association of University Administrators' Oxford branch session • Started work on this book

Table 7.3 (Continued)

Role/grade	Length of time in post	Reason for leaving	Key skills/knowledge acquired	Professional development and other career-enhancing activities
College Registrar (SP37–43), St Antony's College, University of Oxford	Current	n/a	• Core registry functions from recruitment/admissions to graduation • Consolidation of aforementioned skills and knowledge	• Elected to Chair of Governing Body. • Multiple trainings, e.g. chairing governing bodies, implementing new policies, strategic planning, leadership development • Presented at Association of University Administrators' development and skills conference • Presented at Association of University Administrators' national conference • External consultancy project for a national scholarship programme

your networks to advance your career by meeting people in roles more senior than yours to learn how those roles operate and what skills you need to do them. However, career planning can also be about being in a better place to understand your interests, your aims and your circumstances and being ready to grab opportunities whenever they come along. It's been described as 'planned happenstance' – having things in place, so that you are ready to respond when opportunities appear and are willing to do so (see http://plannedhappenstance.com).

You may also want to consider your route through higher education administration – does it take a more generalist or more specialist way forward? For example, Cambridge University's career development programme (see www.skills.cam.ac.uk/staff/career) uses job families to group similar role types together and, within each, covers a range of 'technical' skills and behavioural attributes that they would expect people in those job families to be working towards. Warwick University locates teams and departments in four 'professional service networks' (see http://www2.warwick.ac.uk/services/registrar/networks) students and academic services, strategy and governance, institutional resources and campus and commercial services, but it emphasises the fluidity and cross-boundary nature of the thematic set-ups.

Another reason for doing at least some career planning is because you will find it more difficult to transfer between specialist and generalist areas the more senior you become. Liesl Elder is candid about this:

> It's very difficult to, say, move from Council Secretariat to fundraising. I mean, there are some general administrative roles that are totally transferrable, but as you get into the more senior, highly skilled roles, I think it's quite difficult to transfer skills across general administration. So much of what we [fundraisers] do (and no one likes using corporate terms) is sales and it's a particular skill set, and there's a particular orientation to it that is rare and not everybody likes doing it. Many people would rather swallow glass than talk to someone about money.

Another question that may spring to mind is should one leave the sector to eventually gain a more senior position? This is a difficult question to answer. For some the answer may well be yes, especially if your work is specialist and the skills can be easily transferred – people working in IT, finance, human resources, marketing and so on could all make sensible moves outside of the sector. For more generalist administrators, we don't believe it is quite as straightforward. If you have done your planning and conceptualised your skills and knowledge gaps, it may be that scanning of commercial job opportunities will throw up positions that would serve your purposes; but it may be hard to prove to commercial organisations the value of the skills you've gained. However, there is more likelihood of moving to a third sector organisation which has similar values to universities making the 'match' more logical and it would still give you a different set of experiences. If you have made this move, or you currently work in the commercial sector, then moving *into* universities is probably easier. In the last perhaps eight years or so, there has been a drive to recruit staff with more commercial experience, especially in areas such as business development, corporate communications and external market intelligence. Getting back in probably wouldn't be as hard, as your new skills are likely to be well regarded.

Career paths

As we have noted above, career paths are not necessarily linear and there are multiple different ways to middle and senior management roles, if this is your aim. Here the three authors, who are at different stages in their careers so far, outline their own 'career maps' to date to highlight these differences (Tables 7.1–7.3). What you will be able to see from all three examples is that there has been a consistent moving of roles, either internally or externally, a lot of professional development along the way and not staying in any role for a great deal of time – five years being the maximum for Emma and Heather, four for Michelle.

What you can see from these three examples is that there is no one right way to do things – there isn't even a single way of doing things. That said, you will notice that Michelle and Heather have had some similar roles but that shouldn't lead to assumptions about 'good' jobs to get experience in, simply that the paths of these two particular people have followed somewhat similar trajectories thus far.

What we wish we'd known at the start is almost 'what is possible?' and 'what do I want to achieve?' so that we could have thought ahead a bit more earlier on, accepting, of course, the key role of serendipity – and being brave – in the evolution of anyone's career.

What can you aspire towards?

Let's now look at some of the most senior roles in the institution to which you might aspire and what they typically involve. We're also honest about the prospect of administrators reaching the very top of the university pecking order. The job terminology used aims to reflect common practice; there will, of course, be local variations.

Vice Chancellor/President

The Vice Chancellor/President is the head of the institution and therefore the chief academic and administrative officer of the University. Most frequently the Vice Chancellor/President is someone with an academic background not an administrative or business one. In the UK at least, the sense that academic leadership is paramount cannot be understated and research by Goodall (2009) argues that world-class scholars, not administrators, make the best leaders of research universities. Occasionally, however, the institutional leader will be recruited to the university from outside of academia; for example, Martin Bean, Vice Chancellor of The Open University (UK) was managing director of education at Microsoft and held executive positions at a number of other software companies before joining The Open University in 2009.

Deputy Vice Chancellor/Vice-President

As the job title suggests, the post-holder deputises for the Vice Chancellor/President and usually holds specific responsibilities of their own. This could include responsibility for line management of other senior staff, chairing university committees, representing the university to particular external bodies or raising its profile more generally. As with Vice Chancellor, it would be very unusual in the UK for this role not to be held by someone with a strong academic profile and background.

Pro-Vice-Chancellor/Vice-President

Most universities have a number of Pro-Vice-Chancellors (PVC)/Vice-Presidents who have strategic oversight of a particular area. These usually include research and teaching either as whole areas or split by discipline (e.g. science/technology and arts/social sciences). It is common for a senior academic from the institution to take on a PVC role, either as a part-time secondment or as a permanent position. That said, Whitchurch (2009) believes that 'blended' professionals may have the possibility to move into a PVC role, particularly if its remit is not directly academic. The examples used above were quality, staffing and institutional development; to that you might add: community engagement, external relations, international development. The background for these roles may be less important than the post-holder's ability to effectively contribute to the university's strategy and have the credibility and vision to do so; that will depend partly on the mission of the institution concerned.

Registrar/Chief Operating Officer

This post-holder is responsible for the administration of the university, reporting directly to the Vice Chancellor and with a number of senior officers reporting to them. These senior officers will head their functional or service area. The Registrar/Chief Operating Officer (COO) has an important role to play in university governance and will commonly act as secretary to most if not all senior university committees. The Registrar/COO contributes to university strategy by implementing the underpinning organisational function that helps the university work towards its mission. The role of Registrar is sometimes combined with that of University Secretary.

University Secretary

The University Secretary usually has responsibility for the governance functions of a university and may be clerk to Council and/or Senate or equivalent (i.e. the university's most senior governing bodies). The University Secretary may also hold responsibility for dealing with access to information, privacy issues, human rights, policy and elections. It is becoming more common for the University Secretary role to be incorporated into a Pro-Vice-Chancellorship with a non-academic responsibility.

Director/Head of service or functional department

Senior administrative officers such as Head of Estates, Chief Information Officer, Director of Development, Librarian or Academic Registrar usually report to the Registrar/COO and have delegated authority for the operational management of particular areas. They will manage both people (usually multiple teams) and budgets, and quite often resources too (library holdings, buildings, etc).

Of course, there is no requirement to aim this high. Higher education administration offers a wide range of career options throughout the pay scales: look at the vast array of posts advertised on the www.jobs.ac.uk website every week. It's just good to know how far you might go....

▶ Decisions, decisions

As we've alluded to above, there will be times in our careers where we have to make decisions on what to do next and evaluate the benefits and costs for us and the risks involved. Your career, which is likely to span somewhere in the region of 40 years (and rising!) or so, will have multiple decision points leading to change, temporary tangents, time out for caring responsibilities and so on. Some things can be planned, some opportunities need to be grabbed and some chances need to be passed by, dependent on where you are and what's important at the time. Case Study 7.1 gives an example of how different types of career-related decision-making have panned out for one of the authors so far.

Hugh Jones also gives a good example:

> I'd got into a rut at one University, was fed up and I was up for a job at another very prestigious university. I decided to say 'no'

for three reasons: culture, interesting current activities, and loyalty. On turning down jobs, I don't recommend people do it too often because you can get a bad reputation, but on the other hand, it's very empowering. I think there is a lesson here that I've seen both ways – when appointing people you are not just selecting from a pool and saying 'I'll have you', you're actually saying – do they want to work for me? It's a sales pitch.

Decisions that are made sometimes turn out to be wrong; this is also OK and it won't hold you back if you need to change roles relatively quickly (as long as this doesn't become a pattern). Alan Burrell talks candidly about his experience:

> It obviously depends on your personal circumstances but some-times it is best to admit that you got it wrong and move on. I remember when I worked for the police; the interview reflected a completely different culture to the culture I found when I arrived on my first day. I went home on the first day and I said 'I have made a big mistake here'; from that day I started to look around for another job. I believe you have to accept that you have made a mistake. I knew if I stayed I could probably never make it right. I could make the best of it, as it paid the mortgage, but I don't think I would be happy doing that. You know when you are not the right person … and I just couldn't see myself spending the next 20 years there. It took about 16 months before I found this job, but I knew it was the right course of action.

Alternatively, some opportunities need to be grabbed even though the timing may not be perfect. For example, one author (see Table 7.1) had only been in a role for 14 months before a secondment opportunity at the next grade and in a very good job arose. Luckily she had an extremely supportive line manager (the importance of this cannot be overestimated, see Chapter 5) who released her for the secondment. The secondment then turned into a permanent role and another step along the career path. One of the authors (see Table 7.3) had to move to Oxford to take up her first role at the University of Oxford and did so (including selling a house) in just six weeks. Michael Di Grappa, currently Vice President, Administration and Finance, McGill Univer-sity in Canada, had, at his previous institution, Concordia University (also in Canada), a ten-month opportunity to act as its CEO, which he describes as

> 'the best of times, the worst of times.' The 10 months in the position were the absolute highlight of my career. It was an intense period,

particularly given the crisis situation in the university following the president's departure and anger directed toward the board of governors. As the CEO, I had to manage the crisis but also lead the university through some difficult obstacles. Chief among this was a projected budget deficit of $18 million for the next fiscal year which we managed to erase.

There was tremendous support from all quarters in getting me through these 10 months. When I returned to my role as vice-president on September 1, 2008, not so much. As I said at the time, people help you move up; no one helps you move back down.

These scenarios may not be ideal for you, your line manager or your family, but if your dream job comes up, then sometimes you just have to look at the bigger picture, take the risk and go for it.

Balancing risk is a key element of career management. For example, one of the authors turned down an opportunity to work in a new area of business, because the role was a fixed-term contract and her employing unit wouldn't hold her permanent job open. That was too risky for her; it may have been fine for someone else.

The role of geography also plays an important part in our careers. There is often only one higher education institution in an area, although major cities can be an exception to this. Most people who reach the very top in their careers have moved around: for example, of the three authors, only one has had their whole higher education career at one institution (which is specialist and large). Another of the authors had to make the decision to work apart from her husband – with two young children – when he moved institutions, until she could find an appropriate role in the area as well. However, whilst moving around enables you to broaden your knowledge of the sector and how things are done in different institutions, it is can be problematic for people with caring responsibilities. School-age children (especially at critical exam times) or elderly relatives often require us to be rooted in a geographic area. Moving is expensive, too, and establishing new friendships takes time. It's not all about work, is it?

There are other types of decision to be made at various times often when caring responsibilities have to come first. With young children (or elderly relatives, horses, an allotment, whatever it may be) to look after and a job to pursue as well as trying to have some other activities in your life, something quite often has to give. Your time is a resource and there's only so much of it. So you need to prioritise some things over others until circumstances change and therefore priorities can change. Anyway, as we stressed in Chapter 3 and, indeed, throughout this book, career success depends on being good at what you do.

If you try to spread yourself too thinly, you will end up lacking focus, being exhausted and not delivering results for your institution; this is the death knell of success.

Powell and Mainiero (1992) noted that workers have two main concerns – concern for career and concern for others. People are always concerned for both, but place different degrees of emphasis on the actions and decisions they take at different times, or try to balance both. Universities as employers are pretty good and generally offer much flexibility in roles and hours, for example, backed up by the Equality Act legislation in the UK. Take advantage of the good employment terms when you need to. It's not a crime to take your foot off the career accelerator to concentrate on other things; you can put it down again at a more suitable time. However, it should be noted here that research evidence from the private sector suggests that both men and women suffer disadvantages when perceived not to be fully committed to work (Stroh and Reilly, 1999, p. 313). What's important, though, is that you make the decision that's right for you.

Jayne Dowden, HR Director at Cardiff University, shared this experience from earlier in her career, before she joined the higher education sector:

> When I went back to work after my first child, I'd had to leave the civil service because you couldn't work part-time at my grade, so I took a job with the Welsh Consumer Council. I was there for about a month and my childcare arrangements were just disintegrating. I spoke to the director and said, 'Look, I'm going to have to leave, I can't do this'. She sat me down and she talked me through various coping strategies, talked me through different options for childcare, talked me through how I could give it a go and actually helped me sort out my life and enabled me to stay in work.

Considering all of the above means that you do need to have some personal resilience. By resilience we mean our ability to adapt and bounce back when things do not go as we planned or hoped. According to Susan Kobasa (see www.mindtools.com/pages/article/resilience), there are three elements that are essential to resilience: challenge, commitment and control. People who show resilience tend to view a difficulty as a challenge, not as a paralysing event. As mentioned previously, they learn lessons from failure and continue to learn and grow; they do not see it as a negative reflection on their self-worth.

Resilient people are also committed to their personal and career goals: they spend their time focussed on events that they can control and do not waste time trying to control events over which they have no control. At some point or another, you will get turned down for a job you really want and you will make mistakes along the way, but this is part of the dynamic learning process. Indeed, one of the unexpected things we learned whilst researching this book is that senior administrators may well be found at the end of a conference dinner playing 'worst mistake top trumps'! If you never made any mistakes, you wouldn't be learning new things or taking on new challenges. Use these as learning opportunities; for example, feedback from unsuccessful interviews can be invaluable in pinpointing where you may need to do some more development or gain different types of experience.

Case study 7.1: Emma Sabzalieva, College Registrar, St Antony's College, University of Oxford

Emma Sabzalieva's career path to date is a prime example of that combination of chance, planning, on-the-hoof decision-making and taking opportunities that is probably most realistic for most of us. She joined the UK higher education sector after having worked in Central Asia for an educational charity which was creating a liberal arts undergraduate curriculum to be offered at regional universities.

> Initially, I had very limited knowledge of the objectives of the educational charity I would be working for, having taken the job primarily to move to a Russian-speaking country. But when my contract finished and I was moving back to the UK, I had developed enough interest in the sector to look specifically for jobs in universities. This led me to the Institute of Education, University of London (IoE), initially as a Course Administrator although a year later I successfully applied (with my line manager's encouragement) for an administrative role at the next grade up. Whilst at the IoE, two things outside work happened that have also helped define my pathway since: I had a baby and I studied for a postgraduate certificate with The Open University.
>
> Having then decided to move to Oxford for reasons that neither my husband nor I can quite remember, I found what was at the time my dream job at the University of Oxford working on international postgraduate scholarships. I hadn't meant to leave the IoE quite so soon but this was too good an opportunity to miss.

Emma remained in that role for a whilst, securing promotion via re-grading as part of an internal restructure. Then a secondment opportunity came up at Somerville College to be their Senior Tutor:

> Whilst it was a step up in responsibility and scope, the College was prepared to take a risk on me. Being Senior Tutor is like being Academic Registrar and Personal Tutor in a mini-university of around 500 students, which means you need to become an expert in many aspects of student administration, personnel and governance matters.
>
> After Somerville I went back to a central administration unit and worked on the development of a new student systems programme as well as a project on the professional development of administrators. I then moved to St Antony's College as College Registrar where I enjoy the challenge and fast pace of college life. I'm also chair of a school governing body and have found that developing expertise in school-level educational governance and management has been hugely beneficial for my understanding of education more broadly. I am also developing my academic work through independent research combining my interests in Central Asia, higher education and social change.
>
> So mine has been both a vertical and a horizontal career path so far because I have been forging my own version of a work-life balance. For me, that means being able to work in progressively more senior roles and/or broaden/deepen my experience, whilst being able to pursue lifelong learning and research and family life at the same time. It's about building a career that doesn't just mean 'job', but that takes on a more holistic and meaningful definition. That might not be a balance that works for everyone, but it (just about) works for me.

The work–life balance debate

As we've discussed, productivity is key, not just being busy: you need to be able to prioritise your time to be able to accomplish your tasks in the most efficient way possible. One of the keys to managing this is to have a job that truly motivates you – the desire to get to work and achieve things is unbounded if you love what you're doing. If you don't, and I'm sure many of us have been there, going to work is another chore. As Case Study 7.1 highlights, work-life balance means different things for different people and at different times; the three authors, for example, cannot necessarily differentiate easily between what is 'work' and what is 'life' – the boundaries are blurred and we like it that way (most of the time, at least). Pattison (2013) talks instead of work-life integration. She argues that work is part of life, not separate from it, and that this is actually an advantageous way to think. We think this is a positive approach: if we see work as somehow separate from life how could we possibly achieve the elusive work-life balance? If we have jobs we're motivated by and enjoy, then that means that we are always engaged even outside of the office hours that most of us still have to keep.

▶ Conclusion

We've reached the end of our exploration of the idea of a career and how to manage it for higher education administrators. We hope you agree with us that it is possible to have a fulfilling and successful career for ourselves, whilst working to deliver all the benefits that universities provide.

In this book, we have covered some practical activities that you can undertake to develop your career: understanding the benefits of mentoring and coaching, expanding and working your networks, the importance of good line management, getting qualified and up-skilled, reflecting on your skills and developing professional development plans and understanding all of this in context of the idea of a university itself.

We are lucky to work in a sector that values its people and spends time and money developing us. On top of that we get to work along-side academics, who are often fizzing with new ideas and engaged in their teaching and research – and we get to help and support that endeavour for the public good. We get to help our students, facilitate the development of new ways of teaching and provide support for research and scholarship. We get to work autonomously a lot of the time. By engaging with the work of the university, under-standing our academic colleagues' endeavours as well as finding new and creative ways to support them and using this to improve our own practice, we help professionalise the administration of higher education – how could we not conclude this is the best sector in which to work?!

▶ Next steps

We'll finish up here with some take-away messages distilled from the previous chapters and leave you now to do your 'homework' – to benefit your own career, your institution and the wider sector.

Action list: Junior colleagues
- Get your first degree or your Master's/research project experience
- Ensure you know what specific qualifications you need (e.g. Chartered human resource professional, Chartered accountant)
- Join a professional body
- Write down what you want to achieve in the next year and set realistic objectives
- Develop a professional development plan to make sure this happens
- Talk to your line manager (or mentor/coach) about what you can do to achieve them
- Get a mentor/coach if you can
- Write down your current priorities and try to know if you would be able to meet them
- Reflect on your personal brand and start building the one you want
- Expand your networks
- Manage your online presence
- Volunteer for additional projects to gain experience

Action list: Middle career colleagues
- Get your MBA or other professional qualification
- Make sure you're the sort of line manager who supports their staff in their career aspirations
- Find a voluntary opportunity to expand your experience
- Develop your five-year plan
- Continuously develop your personal development plan
- Get yourself a more senior mentor
- Reflect on your practice and skills
- Get involved with your professional body

Action list: Senior and aspiring senior colleagues
- Keep your five year plan up-to-date
- Keep an eye on job adverts and review the skills and experience needed for the next step
- Continue to take CPD courses to keep your knowledge and skills current
- Mentor more junior staff

- Delegate appropriately to your team, allowing them to make mistakes (and supporting them to fix them)
- Continue to be a reflective practitioner
- Consider professional coaching
- Contribute to the professionalisation of HE administration through your professional body or in other ways
- Remember to help develop the more junior talent in the organisation

▶ References

Burke, J. M. and Attridge, M. (2011) 'Pathways to career and leadership success: Part 2 – striking gender similarities among $100k professionals', *Journal of Workplace Behavioural Health*, 26(3), 207–239.

Cuthbert, R. (1996) *Working in Higher Education*, Buckingham, SRHE/Open University Press.

De Pater, I. E., Van Vianen, A. E. M. and Bechtoldt, M. N. (2010) 'Gender differences in job challenge: A matter of task allocation', *Gender, Work and Organization*, 17(4), 433–453.

Goodall, A. H. (2009) *Socrates in the Boardroom: Why Research Universities Should be Led by Top Scholars*, Princeton and Oxford: Princeton University Press, 13.

Heslin, P. A. (2003) 'Self- and other-referent criteria in career success', *Journal of Career Assessment*, 11(3), 262–286.

Lyness, K. S. and Thompson, D. E. (2000) 'Climbing the corporate ladder: Do female and male executives follow the same route', *Journal of Applied Psychology*, 85(1), 86–101.

Pattison, L. (2013) 'Goodbye work-life balance: Let's embrace work-life integration', *Huffington Post*, www.huffingtonpost.co.uk/lindsay-pattison/worklife-balance-goodbye_b_3580801.html, accessed 26 August 2013.

Powell, G. N. and Mainiero, L. A. (1992) 'Cross-currents in the river of time: Conceptualizing the complexities of women's careers', *Journal of Management*, 18(2), 215–237.

Stroh, L. K. and Reilly, A. H. (1999) 'Gender and careers: Present experiences and emerging trends', in Powell, G. N. (ed.), *Handbook of Gender and Work*, Sage Publications Inc. Thousand Oaks.

Whitchurch, C. (2009) 'Who do they think they are? The changing identities of professional administrators and managers in UK higher education', *Journal of Higher Education Policy and Management*, 28(2), 159–171.

Index